NOT AGAINST FLESH AND BLOOD

The battle against spiritual
wickedness in high places

NOT AGAINST
FLESH AND BLOOD

The battle against spiritual
wickedness in high places

NOT AGAINST
FLESH AND BLOOD

The battle against spiritual

wickedness in high places

DR MARTYN LLOYD-JONES

BRYNTIRION PRESS

CHRISTIAN
HERITAGE

Dr. Martyn Lloyd-Jones (1899-1981) was born in Wales. He was a dairyman's assistant, a political enthusiast, debater, and chief clinical assistant to Sir Thomas Harder, the King of England's Physician. But at the age of 27 he gave up a most promising medical career to become a preacher... When a spiritual history of the 20th century comes to be written it will be bound to include mention not only the far-reaching influence of Dr. Lloyd-Jones' ministry at Westminster Chapel in London, England from 1938-68, but of the remarkable fact that his published volumes of expository sermons have had an unprecedented circulation for such material, selling in millions of copies.

All Scripture quotations, unless otherwise indicated, are taken from the King James version, KJV.

Copyright © Martyn Lloyd-Jones 2012

paperback ISBN 978-1-84550-735-0
epub ISBN 978-1-78191-073-3
mobi ISBN 978-1-78191-074-0

10 9 8 7 6 5 4 3 2 1

First published in 2001, reprinted in 2013
by
Christian Focus Publications,
Geanies House, Fearn,
Ross-shire, IV20 1TW, Scotland
www.christianfocus.com
with
Bryntirion Press
Pen-y-bont ar Ogwr/Bridgend
CF31 4DX, Wales, Great Britain

Cover design by DUFI-ART.com

Printed by Bell and Bain, Glasgow

MIX
Paper from
responsible sources
FSC® C007785

Contents

CONTENTS

FOREWORD

The sad but often well-deserved fate of most authors is the almost certain demise of their books soon after their own death. This seems particularly true of those authors thought to be most current and contemporary in their own day. The *au courant* author of one decade is usually forgotten in the next.

This makes the influence of Dr. Martyn Lloyd-Jones all the more remarkable. 'The Doctor', as he was fondly known, died on the first day of March in 1981, but his books remain as popular and influential as ever. Indeed, The Doctor's literary output after his death has outpaced what he knew during his long and illustrious ministry, spanning almost thirty years at London's famous Westminster Chapel.

This powerful volume, *Not Against Flesh and Blood*, is a prime example of the power and enduring relevance of The Doctor's ministry. It is robustly biblical, thoroughly orthodox, spiritually urgent, and theologically sound. Beyond these qualities, the book stands out for its brave and timely consideration of spiritual warfare—one of the most timely concerns in the present hour of Christianity.

Martyn Lloyd-Jones was both a physician and a physician of souls, and both are on display in this book. Trained as a medical doctor, Dr. Lloyd-Jones served as assistant to the King's own physician. When he entered the Christian ministry and took up the call to preach, many must have wondered if that precious medical education would be wasted. *Not Against Flesh and Blood* answers that question, and it does so decisively.

This book could only have been written by one who possessed both medical and theological wisdom. As a physician, The Doctor knew how to deal with scientific evidence. When it came to evidence of spiritism and its phenomena, The Doctor affirmed the existence of real demonic possession and activity. 'They are not all fraudulent,' he explained. He affirmed the reality of 'certain phenomena that cannot be explained' without the existence and actions of evil spirits.

At the same time, he asserted that 'it is never a part of Christianity to deny facts.' To the contrary: 'You do not strengthen the Christian case by simply dismissing something – I am referring to facts, not theories – it is not only not scientific to deny facts, it is not Christian. Christianity faces facts and does not care where they come from, whether from science or some other source. We must never base our position on obscurantism, upon a refusal to face well-attested facts.'

Writing against the background of the revival of the occult in the 1960s and 1970s, The Doctor called upon the church to face the very real fact that a genuine spiritual warfare was now at hand. He also explained that the reason for this revival of the occult was the increasing secularity of the age—an age later described as post-Christian.

The revival did not surprise The Doctor, who rooted it in an education 'that becomes purely secular and denies the Bible entirely and denies God and becomes atheistical'. He described the British society of his day and diagnosed the problem. As he asserted, 'in an age of moral declension, in an age of godlessness, in an age of excesses, in an age when people no longer believe in God and begin to dabble with the unseen and to play with evil, invariably this phenomenon comes back'.

In the face of the occult revival, Dr. Lloyd-Jones affirmed the reality of evil and the demonic. In this important book, he traces the threat of evil back to the Fall in Genesis 3, declaring, 'The Fall alone explains why men and women are as they are, the slaves of sin and the devil.'

While many of his fellow evangelicals located the problem of sin only at the level of the individual, The Doctor affirmed the existence and threat of magnified evil in human institutions as well. Against secular utopians and their hope for an end to evil through international action, The Doctor declared that human efforts to eliminate war and violence through international bodies are 'temporary expedients that always come to nothing'. In his view, all these efforts came to 'simply turning round and round in a circle'.

At the same time, The Doctor expressed total confidence in the Gospel of Jesus Christ, and in the total victory of Christ over the devil and his demons. Dr. Lloyd-Jones rightly understood that the singular means of liberation from the powers of darkness is conversion to Christ. The one who is found in Christ cannot be possessed by a demon.

The Doctor's medical training serves an important role in this book. Looking at the phenomena of demonic activity, he carefully defined the evidence of demonic possession and distinguished it from medical disease. Thus, he corrects the assumption on the part of the boy's father in Matthew 17, who believed that his son was an epileptic, who repeatedly threw himself into fire. As Dr. Lloyd-Jones noted, such deliberately self-destructive behavior is foreign to any medical definition of epilepsy. It was, he insisted, evidence of purely demonic activity. Similarly, The Doctor credited another trained physician, Luke, for drawing the right contrast between the medical and the demonic in Luke 4:40-41. 'The Bible draws a clear and scientific distinction between diseases, devil possession, and lunacy,' he asserted. 'There is no confusion.'

Martyn Lloyd-Jones did not want his people to be confused about anything. His preaching was a passionate display of biblical and doctrinal clarification. He pointed all persons to Christ as the only remedy for sin and all its effects. He grounded his teaching in the full authority of Scripture, and he was a meticulous interpreter of the biblical text.

The Doctor was fully confident of the defeat of the devil, the demons, and the entire empire of evil. He knew that Christ would display his total victory in due time, on the arrival of the Day of the Lord.

Until then, he knew that Christians need to understand the reality of the demonic and the nature of the spiritual warfare to which every Christian is called.

I never had the opportunity to hear The Doctor preach in person. I greatly regret that I never heard his living voice or had the privilege of meeting him. Nevertheless, I have listened to hundreds of hours of his preaching and teaching in recorded form. Having done so, I am well aware that The Doctor's writings bear the same marks as his preaching. I can almost hear his voice as I read these words.

Not Against Flesh and Blood is an important book, no less now than when it was first delivered as messages to a living congregation over thirty years ago. I celebrate this new edition, and I am honored to introduce it to a new generation – a generation in urgent need of its message.

This book contains a wealth of spiritual teaching, and it is a great encouragement to the church in any age. Why? Because the church is always engaged in spiritual warfare, and will be until Jesus comes.

R. Albert Mohler, Jr.,
The Southern Baptist Theological Seminary, Louisville, Kentucky

The Doctor was fully confident of the defeat of the devil, the demons, and the entire empire of evil. He knew that Christ would display his total victory in due time, on the arrival of the Day of the Lord.

1

THE FORCES OF EVIL AND THE NATIONS

'We wrestle not against flesh and blood, but against principalities, against powers, against the rulers of the darkness of this world, against spiritual wickedness in high places.' (Eph. 6:12)

Nothing is made so plain and clear in the teaching of the New Testament as the fact that the Christian is 'a new man'. Christians are not merely good men and women, they are not merely better than others, they are essentially new people. What makes us Christians is that we undergo rebirth. As a result, we become partakers of the divine nature, the life of God enters into our souls and the Holy Spirit dwells within us.

The New Testament constantly emphasises the fact that, as the apostle Paul puts it, 'If any man be in Christ, he is a new creature [a new creation]' and the result is that 'old things are passed away; behold,' Paul says, 'all things are become new' (2 Cor. 5:17).

That is the great characteristic of Christian people. Everything is new. Because they have a new mind, they have a new outlook, a new orientation, they see things in an entirely new way. Their attitude towards everything around them is influenced by this profound change that has taken place within them, and their reaction to all that happens is, of necessity, different from the reaction of other people. Consequently, anything that happens to Christian men and women immediately becomes a test of who they are and what they believe as Christians.

REMEMBRANCE SUNDAY

We who are Christians therefore view a day like this—Remembrance Day, as we have come to call it[1]—in an entirely different way from all who are not Christians. We are in the same world as everybody else, subject to the same events, the same accidents. Like everybody else we are citizens of this earthly kingdom, but we have our own particular view of this day of remembrance. A day like this comes as a test to those of us who claim to be Christians. What does it mean to us? How should we observe it? What is its message to us? What is its meaning? What does it really represent?

Ways of remembering

Now there are many possible ways of reacting to Remembrance Day. There are many different ways in which it can be observed and many different ways of

---

1   Remembrance Day is held annually in Britain to commemorate those who died in the two world wars.

conducting a Remembrance Day service in a Christian church. Such a service can be a purely formal occasion without any real life or spiritual content. Even in a church it can be observed in the way that the world outside observes it, but with the addition of a kind of religious veneer. It can be essentially something national, an opportunity for pride and self-congratulation. It can be nothing but an occasion for mourning or for thanksgiving. It can be a time when people consider the international situation and express their views on international politics, on what should be done or not done, and work out the various ramifications of armaments talks and peace negotiations.

The Christian way

I want to suggest that the truly Christian way of approaching Remembrance Day is the way that is indicated in these words that we are looking at together. Here is the spiritual approach, and not only that, it is, at the same time, of course, the only radical, the only deep way of approaching this subject. Now that is what we claim for the teaching of the New Testament, for the Christian gospel. We claim that the outstanding characteristic of the biblical view of the whole of life and of human history is its profundity. It is never content with looking at things on the surface; it is not mere observation. It does not give the obvious answers and explanations and it is never concerned merely about the clichés. It goes down to the very depths. All the talk of the philosophers and the psychologists has been made ridiculous by the history of this twentieth century. The Bible, and the Bible alone, raises the fundamental questions, and it alone has an adequate answer to those questions.

So I suggest that here, in Ephesians 6, we find the true way of approaching the Day of Remembrance. Here the apostle leads us to the very heart of the matter for here he lays down the great proposition that this world of ours, and the whole course of human history, is, in the last analysis, nothing but the arena in which a mighty spiritual conflict is taking place, a conflict between God and the forces of heaven, and the devil and the forces of evil and of hell. 'We wrestle not against flesh and blood, but against principalities, against powers, against the rulers of the darkness of this world, against spiritual wickedness in high places.'

And that, according to the Bible, is the ultimate explanation of the whole of human history, both biblical and secular.

THE ORIGIN OF EVIL IN THE WORLD

In the Bible we are given the true teaching with regard to the origin of evil, the origin of the devil and of these principalities and powers. In the great story of the Fall we see how these powers and forces first entered into human history. We see how the devil came and tempted Adam and Eve and how, in their folly, they listened and fell. And we see how, as the result of that fall, the devil and these powers have been dominating the life of humanity.

We cannot understand the world today without the doctrine of the Fall. The Fall alone explains why men and women are as they are, the slaves of sin and of the devil. The devil is the god of this world and, by nature, we are in the kingdom of darkness.

The devil and his forces exert their power upon us first and foremost by attacking our minds, but not only our minds, they attack our moral nature and, indeed, even our bodies. And the devil does not confine his attacks to individuals.[2] It is an essential part of the teaching of the Bible that he operates on a world-wide scale, with larger groupings—states, nations and continents. All this raises the whole question of the occult, spiritism and devil possession

A world at war

We are all aware of the state of the world at the moment. We hear of horrible armaments being piled up. Are we on the brink of a third world war? These are the thoughts that are in everybody's minds, so let us see how the Bible approaches the subject of war. Let me summarise the principles which are taught here in Ephesians 6 and in the whole Bible with regard to a day like this, a day of remembrance, a day in which we remember particularly the two world wars that have taken place within this one century.

The causes of war

First, why do wars happen at all? The tragedy today is that people do not seek the causes. They are so bemused by particular symptoms and manifestations

---

2   For Dr Lloyd-Jones' sermons on this subject, see *The Christian Warfare, Ephesians 6:10-13*, Banner of Truth Trust, 1976.

that they proceed at once to them and try to apply their remedies. Instead of looking for the cause, they talk about armaments and things like that. But the Bible is concerned with root causes, fundamental explanations. Now what are they?

Here is the answer: 'We wrestle not against flesh and blood.' The first principle given to us by the Bible is that, contrary to general opinion, the causes of war are not to be found only in people.

'Ah,' someone says, 'if the Kaiser hadn't lost his head, we would never have had the First World War. If it hadn't been for Hitler, or Stalin, or Kruschev ...' That is the mentality of the politicians and of the vast majority of people.

No, says the Bible. 'We wrestle not against flesh and blood.' It is not human beings.

Many others think that the whole problem is purely economic. Some say, 'If it were not for Communism, all would be well!', while others say the same thing about capitalism! They agree that if only we could deal with the fundamental problem of economics things could be put right.

Not so, according to this Book, because economics is still a human problem.

Nor do wars come about merely for political reasons. Politics comes in, of course, all these issues play a part, but they are merely the things that are used. No, our conflict is not against flesh and blood. These evils are entirely the result of the operation of the devil and the principalities and powers, the rulers of the world, the rulers of this darkness, this spiritual darkness, in high places, in the heavenlies. They are all the work of the devil as he operates both upon individuals and upon larger groupings.

The devil's purpose
Now the one supreme object of the devil is to bring in confusion and chaos. Why? Because God's work is always characterised by order, by perfection. Everything that God does is orderly, it has symmetry, and the devil, filled with pride and antagonism, hating God as he does, is out to destroy God's handiwork. He is, therefore, ever a cause of turmoil, of discord, and confusion, and in that respect, what can he do better than to produce wars? And that is what he has been doing throughout the running centuries. James says, 'Whence come wars and fightings among you?' (James 4:1). And he answers, 'Come they not hence, even of your lusts that war in your members?' This is the work of the devil, playing upon the mind, playing upon the moral nature, to stimulate these unworthy elements in fallen men and women. And so you have the explanation of wars.

The devil's methods
But let me work it out a little. How does the devil bring about wars?

In the first instance, *the devil produces lawlessness.* The devil attacks the mind, and that was the original temptation: lawlessness. When God laid down his law for the man and woman in the garden, the devil immediately queried it. Rebellion! Setting law and order on one side; taking the law into your own hands; doing what you want to do! That is ultimately the cause of every kind of war, including the moral warfare in different countries today. It is the cause of the major problems that confront us. Robberies with violence, murder, and all that fouls the life of a nation, are ultimately due to <u>lawlessness, and that is the devil.</u>

This same lawlessness is found among nations. Disregard for law and for the sanctities of law is the root cause of all wars. People may sign agreements, they may give their solemn pledges at a conference but then, for their own reasons, they suddenly break the promises, take the law into their own hands, and act. Is that not the cause of war? And this lawlessness and rebellion is produced by the devil.

And then, to work it out in a little more detail, *the devil works upon our pride*, both national and personal pride. A prolific cause of all wars throughout the centuries has been just this question of pride. It has been the cause of strife between individuals; it has been the cause of wars between nations. Nations are proud of themselves and of their national sovereignty, and exaggerate their achievements. And that, of course, always leads to jealousy, envy and opposition. If you read secular history books, you will find that pride is one of the greatest causes of war, and it is ever something that is produced by the devil.

Then with pride come *greed and selfishness*. You put yourself first. You feel that you are an exceptional person and that you have a right to all you want. Nations believe that they have a right to possess the whole earth, so they will attack another nation without any provocation, and will conquer and possess it. All this is merely a manifestation of that original pride, that exaggerated notion of self, that puffing up that was the ultimate cause of the fall of the devil himself.

These forces of greed, selfishness and pride ever lead to a *spirit of distrust and uncertainty*. You see a man beginning to set himself up, so you watch him. Then you, in turn, tend to find the same mentality developing in yourself. In this way, the whole atmosphere of war is created.

Now these are the fundamental causes of war. There are foolish people who say it is making the armaments that causes war, but the question is: What makes men make their armaments? Why should they even think of it? You must go back to the radical cause, and there it is!

Biblical case histories

The Bible is full of illustrations of the devil's methods. Here we see psychology, here we see sound philosophy. The first biblical illustration, of course, is Cain. Why are there wars? It is because there are people like Cain. Here were two brothers, Cain and Abel, and without any reason, Cain began to feel jealous of his brother. Now this terrible jealousy was introduced by the devil and the principalities and powers. This is what we are fighting against. He insinuates thoughts into the mind and we are not aware of it. We feel that our country is innocent, that we never do any harm at all, that it is always the other nation. But the other nation is

21

saying exactly the same about us. Cain: There it is in a nutshell.

Then look at the story of Naboth's vineyard. There was King Ahab who had so many great possessions yet wanted Naboth's vineyard. He had no right to it. It was Naboth's little possession, But this great king must have it. He wanted it so desperately that, instigated by his wife Jezebel, he proceeded to take it in an unlawful manner. That is what happens within a nation.

But this lawlessness does not merely happen in individuals and groups, it happens on a wider scale. Look at the people before the Flood as they are described in Genesis 6: the vice, the evil, (which always leads to quarrelling) men and women setting themselves up in pride, turning away from God. Look at the Tower of Babel, another illustration of exactly the same thing. This was the pride of unregenerate, fallen humanity. Look at the wars that Israel had to fight against the other nations. Look at what we read in the Old Testament about great dynasties like Assyria and Babylon, Media, Persia and Rome. Look at the inflated pride of these successive empires that tried to spread themselves over the whole world. They caused wars and turmoils and wretchedness and the unhappiness of the human race.

Demonic power

So far we have been looking at what I would call the general operation of the devil and his forces, the way in which, as it were, he keeps himself in the background but, nevertheless, insinuates ideas into individuals and nations. We must now go a step further because as we look back at both biblical and secular history, quite clearly we see something else that we must call the demonic element. Sometimes we see not merely selfishness and evil and pride and all the rest, but an additional factor.

Let me give you an illustration or two. Take Nebuchadnezzar and the events described in Daniel 4. Nebuchadnezzar was not only inflated with pride and a sense of his own greatness, he went beyond that. He set himself up as a god and demanded people's worship. Now it is just there that the demonic element comes in. That is not mere evil, but something further, a kind of possession; the man gets beyond himself, beside himself.

We find the same thing in Antiochus Epiphanes, again described in the book of Daniel, and known from secular history to have lived in the years between the book of Malachi and the Gospel of Matthew in the times of the Maccabees, that terrible period through which the Israelites, the children of God, had to go. He was another man who demanded worship and set himself up as a god and that is where this something extra, this demonic element came in.

And, of course, we find the same thing in the Roman Empire. These emperors were not only great military conquerors, but they, too, began to set themselves up as gods. This was one of the great battles that the early Christians had to fight. They said, 'Jesus is Lord,' but the Roman Empire said, 'Caesar is lord,' and demanded that the Christians should say that, too. When the Christians refused, they were thrown to the lions in the arena. Emperor worship! That is demonic, it is the only word for it; Caesar, setting himself up for worship and for adoration, turning himself into a god. That is what the devil brought about.

Islam has this same demonic element in it. Here was a man, Mohammed, setting himself up and inflating himself, and that led to so many of the so-called religious wars. And this demonic element has continued to show itself from time to time in the long history of the human race.

Of course, there are many disputed instances. Personally, for example, I would not put Napoleon into this category. I think that his actions can be explained entirely in human terms. I do not think the demonic element was there. He was just an outstanding military genius whose brilliance ran away with him. But there is no doubt about Hitler. Here was a man who demanded an attitude of worship and adoration; a man who was religious, in the wrong sense; a man who worshipped himself, worshipped his own race and worshipped his own administration. He demanded complete control over the minds of men and women, over the whole person. Now that is the demonic element. Napoleon never did that. It is no part of my purpose to defend Napoleon, but it is important that we should be clear about this demonic element and where exactly it comes in.

Undoubtedly, we also see the demonic in a totalitarian system like Communism because Communism does not stop merely at an economic order but really believes in worship of the state. Communism claims the right to determine a person's thinking: scientists have to think within prescribed limits and novelists must write within prescribed terms. Anything that demands the worship of a man, or of a state, or of a system, any totalitarian society that requires total allegiance, is demonic.

To be honest, there have been evidences of the demonic in the history of Great Britain. There are people who are still guilty of it, though they are not aware of it. It has never been an official policy in this country, but in practice and in private it has very often been present. There has been a kind of mystique about the British Empire which, to me, has had demonic elements in it, and that is where we all need to be careful.

GOD'S VICTORY

What, then, according to the Bible, have been God's enactments in the light of this? What has God, as it were, been doing in the light of this activity of the devil and the principalities and the powers, and the world rulers of this darkness, this spiritual wickedness in the heavenly places? Now here we come to the second principle and it seems to me that we can divide the answer into two main sections.

God's temporary measures

I am referring here to the institution of governments and 'the powers that be'. The classic statement of this is in Romans 13:1, 'Let every soul be subject unto the higher powers. For there is no power but of God: the powers that be are ordained of God.'

Because of the influence of the devil and his forces of evil and sin God introduced government, kings, princes and magistrates, and he gave certain powers to them, as Paul puts it: 'For he [the magistrate] beareth not the sword in vain' (v. 4). Governments not only lay down laws, they have the power to enforce them. They are able to demand punishment for lawbreaking. That is the essence of the notion of government.

Now it is the biblical teaching that it is God who has introduced governments. It is not that human beings have gradually developed tribal ideas into the idea of governments as we think of them, but that states and governments are of divine ordination. They are meant to restrain and to keep within bounds these forces of evil and chaos which are ever being enlivened by the activity of the devil and his powers. Here they are, trying to cause dislocation and chaos and turmoil and war, and the business of government is to restrain them, to keep them under control, to preserve law and order and to prevent chaos—that is the essence of biblical teaching.

But there is also another element. Quite clearly God has permitted certain things to happen from time to time. He has allowed certain persons and groups to arise and to arrogate unto themselves almost endless powers. Individuals, nations and empires have made many attempts to dominate the whole world. They have said that they wanted to produce peace and order, but have added that the way to do it is to conquer everything. If everybody is kept down, then there will be no war.

And God has permitted this. He permitted it before the Flood when he allowed those foolish people to begin building their Tower of Babel. They thought that they had all knowledge, that they had encompassed the whole of truth: they were going to build a tower right into heaven. And God let them to build it up to a certain point.

God allowed the Babylonians to build a mammoth empire that looked as if it was going to conquer the whole universe. He allowed Egypt and Alexander the Great and the Median, Persian and Greek dynasties to behave in the same way, and also the Romans with their great Roman Empire. Later Islam and the Turkish Empire looked as if they were going to conquer the whole world.

So here is the interesting teaching: God, in his eternal and inscrutable wisdom, seems to allow these powers and these persons to do these things. They rise up and spread themselves; they, as it were, try to stride the world as though they were some sort of Colossus and, indeed, nothing seems to be able to stop them. On and on they go, the whole world is quaking, and you feel that here, at last, is a man who is a semi-god. But invariably, without a single exception, just when man has arrived at the very zenith of his power, God suddenly arises against him. God pronounces his judgment upon the usurper, brings him down and destroys him and his power.

That is the great story in Daniel chapter 4. Look at this man, Nebuchadnezzar, who stands up as a giant, as a god almost, and demands the worship of the people. Yes, but look at him in a few months: there he is like an ox in a field, eating grass. Look at his nails, they are like talons. Look at his skin, his long hair almost looks like the feathers of a bird. What a fool! What a monstrosity! What has happened to him? Oh, it is God who has just put him in his place, reminding him that there is only one God and that nobody is to be worshipped but God Himself.

Now it is a most interesting fact in human history that God has never allowed any person or any nation or any power or any theory to dominate the whole world. He never will! Let every empire beware. An empire that begins to lose its head and imagines that it is endless and almost divine is as certain to come to destruction as Nebuchadnezzar.

And look at Belshazzar. There he is in his feast with his concubines and his drink. Typical modern potentate, is he not? And what is he drinking from? He is using the vessels taken from the temple of God in Jerusalem. He is using these very holy cups as he enjoys his revelries with his concubines and all his associates. But in the very midst of the feast and the jollifications and the rejoicing about his greatness, there is the hand—the hand and the writing, *MENE, MENE, TEKEL, UPHARSIN*. 'Thou art weighed in the balances and art found wanting.' Your kingdom is judged, you have come to the end (Dan. 5:25-8). And down he goes; that very night his kingdom falls.

And so it is with all of them. Alexander the Great died at an early age of an aneurism. When Rome felt that it was supreme, it was conquered by the Goths and the Vandals and the Barbarians. Turkey likewise was brought down. And what of Egypt today? God permits these powers for a while, but only for a while, He rises—suddenly they are destroyed.

God's ultimate measure

But, of course, God does not merely take temporary measures to overcome evil; he has an ultimate measure. God first announced it in the Garden of Eden. When Adam and Eve fell, God said to the man: There will be warfare between the seed of the serpent and your seed. There will be a terrible fight. 'I will put enmity between thee and the woman, and between thy seed and her seed; it shall bruise thy head, and thou shalt bruise his heel' (Gen. 3:15).

God was introducing his new kingdom. It starts there in the Garden of Eden and it runs on through the Old Testament. Christ came 'when the fulness of the time was come' (Gal. 4:4); it was the bringing in of the kingdom. It will go on until the fulfilment, pictured in the book of Revelation, when 'the kingdoms of this world are become the kingdoms of our Lord, and of his Christ' (Rev. 11:15), when the devil and all his forces will be finally routed, with all who belong to them, and cast into the lake of fire and of burning. That is the ultimate purpose, and it is the great message and theme of the Bible.

So do not confuse the temporary measures and the ultimate measures. God allows these powers to rise— then he brings them down; it is all temporary. But keep your eye on God's ultimate purpose. The kingdom of God, the kingdom of light, the kingdom of heaven is coming. It is being introduced; its citizens are being gathered together. It will continue until the final clash, and Christ, the Prince of Peace and the King of Righteousness, will reign supreme over all.

THE CHRISTIAN'S DUTY

Then the third principle is the Christian's duty in the light and in the midst of all this. Let me just give you some headings.

Avoid and restrain all causes of war

I have talked about some of the causes of war. A Christian never says, 'My country right or wrong.' That is a terrible sin. He is never a party to jingoism.

Refuse to fight in a war of aggression

If their country sets out in an aggressive war to steal another nation's property or land, Christians should refuse to participate. They must never be guilty of this pride in themselves or their nation. They must never be guilty of this selfishness, this greed, this avarice, this evil spirit. They must stand against it.

Resist the forces of evil

Christians are to aid the state and the government that is appointed of God in its task of arresting and subjugating, as far as is possible, the forces of evil. By this I mean that Christians do not contract out of their responsibilities by saying, 'We're Christians, this is not our fight. We'll start a campaign of civil disobedience because we don't take part in war.' They do not say that! They do not take part, let me repeat, in an aggressive war, but I would argue that it is their duty as citizens to take part in a war that is meant to restrain aggression and to punish evil and to keep it within bounds. Pacifism is heresy: it is not Christian teaching.

THE FUTURE OUTLOOK

This brings me to my last principle, and it is obvious, is it not, from what I have been saying?

False optimism

There is nothing more fatuous and ridiculous than the false optimism which followed the First World War in particular. At that time ridiculous, blinded men said that was 'the war to end wars', and people went mad thinking that the League of Nations was going to put an end to war. That is un-Christian and utter spiritual blindness. Anyone who can believe that has never understood the essence of the biblical teaching concerning the Fall.

In 1925, there was great excitement about the Locarno Pact. The politicians thought that at last they had done it: a pact to outlaw war! But we did not have to wait long to see the folly of that, did we? I repeat that a man or woman who believes that any league, union or organisation will banish war has never understood the spiritual teaching of the Bible. They are thinking in terms of flesh and blood, and do not understand human nature. They have no knowledge of the devil and the principalities and powers of evil.

Realism

Men and women will never introduce an era of peace. Nor are we promised it. The Bible says that wars will last as long as human beings are in sin.

You say, 'What terrible pessimism!'

Yes, it is, but it is the truth. It is realism. There is nothing that I know of that is so fatuous as to whip ourselves up into a false optimism, just to feel a little bit happier while we are in a church service before going back to face the world as it is.

No, it was the Son of God who said, 'Ye shall hear of wars and rumours of wars' (Matt. 24:6). And James asks, 'From whence come wars and fightings among you? come they not hence, even of your lusts that war in your members?' (James 4:1). And while there is lust, there will be war. How can you hope to put an end to war when one man has lust towards another man's wife, or covets his possessions? That is war! Nations are nothing but aggregates of individuals.

And there is the demonic element. As long as he has any power, the devil will produce chaos and confusion and antagonism and war.

Again you say, 'What a terrible picture! I wish I hadn't come to this service.'

Is that your attitude? Are you content just to pull down the blinds and not face facts? That is to abdicate responsibility. That is to run away. That is not to use your reason. No, no! Let us face it. Primarily the Bible is pessimistic because it is realistic.

Looking to the future
How, then, do I face the future? As a Christian I face it like this: I expect nothing from men and women. I expect nothing from conferences. I expect nothing from leagues

or united nations organisations—call them what you will. That is why I do not preach about them: I do not want to waste my breath or your time. They are simply turning round and round in a circle. They are temporary expedients that always come to nothing. They are not a part of the spiritual message at all.

So I expect in the future—what? Anything! I shall be surprised at nothing. There may be a period of peace, there may not be. I do not know. Nobody knows. Anything is possible from humanity in sin. There have been long periods of peace, but it is always only temporary. There have been periods of war—the Hundred Years' War, for instance. We may get that in the future. I cannot tell you; we do not know.

The day of the Lord

What I do know is that wars and strife will go on until the arrival of God's appointed day, the day of the Lord. And, oh, here is the optimism, here is the assurance. There is a day, an appointed day, the day of the Lord. There is a definite end to history. I do not know when it will be: I do not understand the times and seasons and the Bible tells me not even to try. All I know is that there is a promised day of God, a day when the Lord Jesus Christ shall come back as the King of kings and the Lord of lords, riding the clouds of heaven, surrounded by the holy angels. And he will destroy every enemy: the devil, the principalities and powers, the very rulers of this darkness, this spiritual wickedness in the high places. They will all be finally destroyed.

Jesus shall reign where'er the sun
Doth his successive journeys run;
His kingdom stretch from shore to shore,
Till moons shall wax and wane no more.

Isaac Watts

A day is coming when war will be no more, when there will be no more sorrow or sighing, when swords will indeed be turned into ploughshares, when the lion will lie down with the lamb. But when will it be? Oh, at the end of history, when Christ ushers in his glorious, eternal kingdom. That is the ultimate outlook because it is God's ultimate plan.

So whatever you and I may have to endure, let us be prepared for it. We may have to go through another war. We may see a world power arising that will persecute us and cast us into prison. We may have to die for the name of Christ as the first Christians did, and as many a Christian has done throughout the running centuries. I do not know! But what I do know is that all who belong to Christ will be with him in that kingdom of glory. This is my interest, this is my concern, and it is a concern that is much greater than my concern about the future of my country. I am interested in my country as a citizen, but above all, I am a citizen of heaven: my citizenship is there, and that is my first concern. I look forward to walking under the new heavens in the new earth 'wherein dwelleth righteousness' (2 Pet. 3:13). I look forward to gazing into the face of the Prince of Peace.

2

THE MANIFESTATIONS OF EVIL POWERS

'Finally, my brethren, be strong in the Lord, and in the power of his might. Put on the whole armour of God, that ye may be able to stand against the wiles of the devil. For we wrestle not against flesh and blood, but against principalities, against powers, against the rulers of the darkness of this world, against spiritual wickedness in high places.' (Eph. 6:10-12)

We are considering the battle that we all have to wage against the powers of evil, the devil and the forces that follow him, and we have seen the influence of these powers over the nations. Now it is no use considering how we are to fight these forces unless we are aware of something of their nature and the way in which they operate. And so we come back again to this large subject, which can be summed up under the technical term, *demonology*.

WHY STUDY DEMONOLOGY?

Now you may be wondering why this subject should be dealt with at all. Are we animated merely by a sense of curiosity? Is it just intellectual interest? Well, I can assure you that we are not! There are many who do have such an interest. This whole question of the occult and of psychic phenomena does make a very fascinating study and a great deal of attention is being paid to it today, but we are not interested in it from that standpoint. We are interested merely as it affects us and our Christian life and living.

To understand the Bible

We are considering this subject, first, because there are so many references in the Bible to these evil forces and powers that there is a sense in which we cannot read the Scriptures intelligently unless we know something about them. Take the book of Daniel: we really cannot make sense of it or realise what God enabled Daniel to do unless we know something about the astrologers and wise men and seers who were called by the emperor of Babylon to solve the problem of his dreams.

The danger of ignorance

But in addition, according to the apostle's specific teaching in Ephesians chapter 6, if we are unaware of these evil powers we will almost certainly be defeated by them. Ignorance is one of the greatest causes of stumbling, and there are many people who are so ignorant of these forces that they become their innocent and unconscious victims.

The Scriptures tell us to prove and to test the spirits: 'Beloved, believe not every spirit,' says the apostle John, 'but try the spirits whether they are of God' (1 John 4:1). We are told that there are two types of spirits: first, the Holy Spirit and the angelic powers who are still obedient to God and who do his behest; but secondly, evil forces and powers and spirits. These are extremely able. The apostle Paul tells the Corinthians that the devil is able to transform himself into 'an angel of light' (2 Cor. 11:14). He is as subtle and as clever as that. We are all exposed to false experiences. We are surrounded by the teaching of various cults; Heresies are always ready to insinuate themselves. So you see the importance of knowing something about these evil forces? It is not a matter of intellectual curiosity, it is essential to the living of the Christian life.

To make sense of history

A further reason is that we cannot read about the pagan nations surrounding the children of Israel without seeing that their lives were characterised by their subjection to these powers. If you want to understand something of the history of antiquity as you find it in the Bible, as well as in secular literature, you must know something about this subject.

Occult forces were also a prominent feature in the Middle Ages and we can read about the medieval attitude to witchcraft which continued even until the eighteenth century. Much of the life of the Middle Ages is to be understood in the light of these beliefs, ideas, creeds, influences and powers that were then so manifest.

To withstand evil forces today

Some unenlightened pagan nations are still subject to these evil forces. We send out missionaries, and if we want to have an intelligent interest in their work we must know something about these forces and powers that operate in the open manner that is described in the Old Testament.

And this leads me to what, for me, is the most important reason of all for studying this subject. Certain tendencies that are becoming increasingly evident in this modern world of ours compel us to consider these matters. Today there is a marked renewal of interest in astrology, spiritism, and various other cults, false teachings and 'doctrines of devils', as the apostle Paul calls them in 1 Timothy 4:1; and as Christian people, we are their targets. They are so specious, so spurious, and make such a pretence of being our friends, that as we value our souls and the health of our Christian lives it is imperative that we should know something about them.

THE STUDY OF DEMONOLOGY

Now as I said, this is a large subject, and I shall therefore merely give a bird's eye view of some of the manifestations of the power of these evil forces. It is also a subject that is extremely difficult to classify. The various books that deal with it all have some sort of classification, but it is quite clear that you cannot have any watertight divisions. One aspect tends to pass over into another, but we cannot help that.

However, as far as I can work it out, the best kind of classification seems to be something like this: first, the general activity of these evil, unclean, spirit forces and powers; second, their unusual activities; third, voluntary submission to these powers; fourth, involuntary submission, or, if you prefer it, dominance by these powers.

THE GENERAL ACTIVITY OF EVIL POWERS

Now these powers of evil operate in many ways, but they have one thing in common: they all tend to work upon one major idea, and that is the desire to know the future.

We all want to know the future. We all ask: Am I going to be happy? What will happen to me? And I have no doubt that that desire is innate in human nature, and that it came about entirely as a result of the Fall. The Fall has made men and women dissatisfied. They feel they were made for something bigger, something better, that something is missing. There is a disease in all of us by nature, and this particularly applies to our attitude to the future. The human race is always looking ahead. We want the future to be better; we want it to be brighter; we want it to be happier.

These evil forces and powers who, of course, are well aware of that longing, play upon it, stimulate it and encourage it. They do this by claiming to be able to forecast the future. Indeed, they go further and claim that they can influence and determine the future. In past centuries that was how they were able to tyrannise individuals and nations: people felt that anyone and anything with such power must be placated, pleased and obeyed. And so these forces exercised their malign and nefarious influence upon the human race.

That, then, is the general characteristic, but let us glance briefly at some of the particular operations of these evil powers.

The soothsayer or seer

Here is a type of individual who claims to have hidden knowledge, an ability to know things about us and to know about the future. We read about these people in various books of the Old Testament. Some were called prophets, and called themselves prophets. They made a livelihood out of the knowledge and exceptional power that they claimed to have; it was their business. People went to them and consulted them.

The whole thing is obviously the result of sin. Sin leads to an inordinate interest in self, to self-centredness and self-importance. That is the reason why we want to know what we are going to be, what is going to happen to us, what great good fortune is coming, and all the brightness of our future.

The modern form of soothsaying, of course, is fortune-telling and all that goes under the heading clairvoyance. Fortune-tellers claim that the future can be foreseen, foretold, catered for, and certain things prevented.

Under this category we must also include what are called 'psychic phenomena'. Some people claim that they have so-called 'psychic powers'. They say that this is not something that they develop or produce but a power that they find they possess. Now let us grant that certain people most definitely do have unusual and exceptional powers. They have what is called 'ESP' or 'extra-sensory perception'. They can tell the number of the next card to be drawn, or they can tell from a distance what someone is thinking.

Mesmerism comes under this heading, and also telepathy, which is the awareness some people have of what is happening to somebody who is dear to them and who may be at the other end of the world. Throughout the long history of the human race there have been people who have claimed to possess, and who have undoubtedly possessed, all these powers. But I am putting them all under the category of demonology because that is what the Bible does.

At the present time a great deal of attention is paid to all this, and these claims have been investigated in a very scientific manner. They have an appearance and a veneer of scientific learning. Now I am not disposed to criticise the investigation of these phenomena. Indeed, I think there is a great deal to be said for it, but only on the condition that we have some standard by which to evaluate them. And the tragedy is that so many who are doing the evaluating have no standard at all. They do not have the standard of the Scriptures, for the Scriptures prohibit all these things, as we see in the book of Deuteronomy.

The astrologer

Astrology, again, is a very ancient cult, and it is returning as an influence in this modern world of ours. What does it mean? Well, in its essence it teaches that our lives are influenced and determined very largely by the influence upon us of the stars and the heavenly bodies. We see this in the book of Daniel, where we read that Nebuchadnezzar consulted 'the magicians, and the astrologers ... ' (Dan. 2:2).

There is no doubt as to the origin of this teaching— it is sheer paganism. It reverts back to the belief that every one of the stars was a god, a divine or heavenly power, and that each one of them was able to influence people in the world. The stars are above us, they look down upon us, so a primitive people, sunk in the degradation that followed the Fall, began to think that the stars were gods.

Now that is not put so crudely today, but the foolish, childish, pathetic notion has persisted that somehow or another these heavenly bodies have an influence over us and that it is therefore very important to know under which star you were born. It is thought that the month in which you were born will influence you and determine your character. And there are people who rush avidly to the popular newspapers just to see what the stars say will happen to them in the coming day. Astrology! It is growing in popularity, and people are making fat livings out of the exercise of this extraordinary, pathetic and crude belief. I leave it at that.

But what is so interesting is that in an age like this, which claims to be sophisticated and too intelligent to be Christian, and which is faintly amused at people who still go to places of worship, so many are returning to this kind of belief. It is astonishing to discover people of eminence and ability who really believe that there is something in astrology. It just reveals the emptiness of the soul apart from God; it shows how people in sin and in their unease will clutch at anything that seems to give them hope and a sense of security.

Black magic

Now black magic was part of the life of all the ancient nations. It was a terrible problem in the ancient pagan world and was rampant, of course, in the Middle Ages. In the Bible it makes an appearance in the biblical account of Moses in Egypt. Witchcraft comes under this heading, and is listed by the apostle Paul in Galatians 5 as one of the works of the flesh.

Black magic is not simply a matter of knowledge and of foreseeing and foretelling, but is a claim to some unusual power and to an ability to do certain things. Now ordinary magic shows its cleverness, its ability, its subtlety, in manifestation; but black magic goes beyond that. It claims that it is given a power by some unseen spirit, some unseen influence.

Those who practise it claim something like this: that by the use of certain means—sometimes a stick, sometimes a crystal, and sometimes the organs of various animals—they are able to arrive at a knowledge of matters of vital interest and importance.

Let me give you a quotation from the book of Ezekiel, chapter 21, verse 21: 'For the king of Babylon stood at the parting of the way, at the head of the two ways, to use divination'—he wanted to know what to do and there he stood at the parting of the ways and there he used this divination; 'he made his arrows bright'—arrows or sticks were used: it was believed that when they were shot or thrown, then the powers would determine the direction, like turning a wheel, or spinning something and waiting to see where it stops; 'he consulted with images'—here he probably used mirrors, or something which had belonged to someone now dead who had claimed some unusual occult power; 'he looked in the liver'—it was believed that some extraordinary power resided in the liver. An animal would be killed and its liver removed and examined, and it was claimed that instruction and knowledge was given from the liver's shape and texture.

Now this idea has persisted throughout the centuries. People have believed in the magical power of different organs of the body. So you take them from an animal and apply them to a person to get rid of a disease or a spell, and so on: that is a part of witchcraft. People claimed superhuman power. They claimed to be able to travel from place to place without walking. Furthermore, they claimed that they could influence others, that they could cast spells upon animals, and upon human beings, and even upon inanimate objects.

Why am I giving you all these details? One reason is that these are the kinds of things that have held the human race in bondage, and one of the most glorious victories of Christianity has always been to deliver people from belief in them and from the influence of these unseen powers and forces. I am old enough to remember the vestiges of such beliefs: the idea that some people had the power to cast a spell, the power to turn cream sour, the power to influence an animal in giving birth, and still more, of course, the power to influence human beings. People would believe that they were under a spell that had been cast upon them and would spend their days in misery.

Practitioners of black magic claim, further, that they can heal diseases and cure people from sicknesses. Now there is no question that sometimes they can do this, though I would raise the question of what exactly they are curing, whether an organic condition or merely some imaginary or functional state. But they can produce certain phenomena, and the result is that they can tyrannise men and women.

Now there are countries, nations and peoples today who are held in bondage by black magic. Here is one of the mightiest arguments for the missionary enterprise. Furthermore, in this country, in spite of our education and supposed scientific knowledge, people are going back to these things. And it is only Christianity, only the power of the gospel, that can give deliverance.

THE UNUSUAL ACTIVITY OF EVIL POWERS

Here, again, we come to a most extraordinary subject. I am referring to things about which we read occasionally in the newspapers and which can sometimes be a very real problem: phenomena like poltergeists, ghosts and haunted houses.

Now it is no part of Christianity to deny facts, and there are certain facts that, it seems to me, are well established. These phenomena have been investigated by the Society for Psychical Research, among others, and there can be no doubt but that certain unusual things do happen at times. For instance, you hear about people whose lives have been made impossible because inanimate objects have begun to move in their home. I mention this because I know of a very well-authenticated case that happened to a Christian minister and was entirely solved by the application of Christian teaching. It sounds ridiculous, does it not? But it literally happened. Chairs would move; pictures would fall off the wall; other objects would be found moving in the house; noises would be heard, rappings upon the wall, and so on.

Again, you will have read of haunted houses and heard of people who have claimed to have seen appearances—let us call them ghosts. Now I know that a large number of these have been explained quite simply as the result of the investigations of the Society for Psychical Research. But there remain a few which they cannot explain and which their scientific investigators are prepared to grant as being beyond their understanding. Well, of course, it is beyond their understanding because in the main they do not believe in 'principalities' and 'powers', in 'the rulers of the darkness of this world', in 'spiritual wickedness in high places'. We are told in the Scriptures that there are such powers and that they are able to do these unusual things. Why? Nobody knows! But the fact that there are such phenomena, it seems to me, is entirely beyond any reasonable dispute.

You say, 'Well, I've never seen anything like that.'

Perhaps you have not. There are many things that you and I do not know.

There are more things in heaven and earth, Horatio,
Than are dreamt of in your philosophy.

Hamlet

The mere fact that we, thank God, may not have experienced them, does not mean that they do not exist.

Such unusual manifestations of evil powers go beyond fortune-telling and astrology. Here something is happening that is altogether apart from human agencies. Non-human powers are doing these things and thus creating problems. And that brings me to my third general heading.

VOLUNTARY SUBMISSION TO EVIL POWERS

Now this refers to a subject that is normally called spiritualism, but should be called spiritism. At the present time it is perhaps the most important aspect of demonology. Somehow or another people have the notion that those who have been in this world before us can still influence it and can help us. It stems from the inordinate desire for knowledge of the future, for my well-being, and my self-concern, a desire that all should go well. I cannot do anything about this; well, what if the spirits of the departed can help?

The history of spiritism

The first thing we must realise is that, in spite of what some people may say, there is nothing new about spiritism. It has been going on right through the known history of the human race. You will find a great deal about it in the Old Testament. Necromancers (people who consult the dead) are denounced in

Deuteronomy 18:10-14; in fact, all the practices I have been speaking about are forbidden in that passage: soothsaying, fortune-telling, consulting images, astrology, witchcraft and consulting departed spirits.

As we read the history of pagan nations, we find that they indulged in spiritism to a very great extent. The ancestor worship of Confucianism is, I believe, a part of this selfsame belief, though expressed differently. It is, however, true that spiritism did die down for a considerable length of time, especially after the Protestant Reformation. It is a most wonderful proof of the power of the teaching of the Bible that when the light of the knowledge concerning the Holy Spirit came in, spiritism went out, and there was a period when very little was heard about it.

Unfortunately, a new interest returned in the nineteenth century. My friends from the United States will forgive me for pointing out that it started in the United States about 1843. In that year, in a town in New York State, people in a religious meeting began to shake and tremble. This curious phenomenon persisted, and the people were given the name 'Shakers'. Then in 1848, the daughters of a man called John D. Fox, who lived in Hydeville in New York State, began to exhibit certain phenomena. It is from both these sources that the modern interest and craze in spiritism began.

Interest spread very rapidly. These phenomena were written and talked about to such an extent that people began to feel that they must discover the truth. Was it all bogus? Was it a pretence? Was there something in it? As a result, in 1882 the Society for Psychical

Research was set up in England, and a similar society in the United States in 1888.

But, of course, it was the First World War that gave spiritism its greatest impetus. During that time certain prominent men became believers in it. A chemist, Sir William Crooks, who was undoubtedly an unusually able scientist, became a firm adherent, as did Sir Oliver Lodge, a great physicist, and that able man, originally a doctor and then a novelist, Sir Arthur Conan Doyle.

Now these three men were sincerely convinced of the truth of spiritism, and it was as a result of their books that it became so widespread. These beliefs have even come into the Church, which has set up its own society for the investigation of psychic phenomena. Today spiritism is believed in very widely; it has churches and journals and there are devotees in all ranks of society.

The appeal of spiritism
The main desire, of course, is the desire for comfort. Very many men were killed in the First World War, leaving fathers, mothers, widows, children. Now there is nothing more natural, more instinctive, than the desire for comfort, and especially the desire to know whether the beloved is all right. These young soldiers had been taken suddenly; it was not that they had got old or died as the result of a disease. Abruptly a husband or son was cut off. And, oh, the absence, the desire to know what was happening and, still more, the desire for continuing fellowship! And here was a teaching that said it was possible. Imagine a young

widow, perhaps left with children or the responsibility of running a business. She had relied upon her husband, but suddenly he had gone. If only he could still guide her and help her!

It is my duty to put these things before you because even within the Christian Church there is a society which supports spiritism. The secretary, an ordained clergyman in the Anglican Church, has written a book in which he does not hesitate to say that a belief in psychic phenomena is essential if one really wants to understand and believe the Bible. He writes that as a theological student he was trained to dismiss most of the Bible, especially everything to do with the supernatural. He was a typical, liberal, modernist in his theology. But since becoming a spiritist, or, as he would say, a spiritualist, he has come to understand the Bible in a way that he never could before.

As a student at theological college, this man ridiculed all he read in the Old Testament about angels suddenly appearing to Abraham or to Jacob. Angels? No such things! Utter rubbish! But he says that now, of course, he has no difficulty at all in accepting these stories. In his spiritualistic circles he has seen materialisations. He still does not believe in angels, but he believes in spirit forces that can materialise. So he is now able to accept that 'angels' appeared to Abraham and ascended and descended the ladder in Jacob's dream. He had thought that when Jacob struggled with the angel at Peniel, he was merely suffering from an overwrought imagination; he was in a psychological, if not a psychopathic state. But now, thanks to spiritism, this clergyman can see that Jacob was an unusually psychic person with the power to produce materialisations. There was undoubtedly some personality there with whom Jacob struggled. Moreover, the prophets were also psychic individuals, natural mediums.

Spiritist teaching becomes most serious when it turns to our blessed Lord himself. It is held that our Lord was an exceptionally psychic person. He had the ability to communicate with the unseen realm to an unusual degree, and more than anybody else—hence his authority, hence his miracles, hence his power to foretell the future.

Some advocates of this teaching say that at last they understand and can believe in the resurrection of Christ and his post-resurrection appearances. They never used to be able to believe, and thought it was nonsense. They used to say that Christ did not rise literally from the grave or come into a room and appear to people. But now, they say, thanks to the spirit phenomena, they do believe. Of course spirit bodies can do that sort of thing.

And then at Pentecost, we are told, the followers of our Lord suddenly entered a psychic state, some more than others. And the power claimed for the apostles was nothing but the extraordinary power that psychic people have. This is also the explanation of subsequent events in the church: revivals, people with unusual preaching power, and other gifts.

The promises of spiritism

It is said that if we believed the teaching of spiritism we would get rid of many of our problems. As we have seen, the claim is that through these people called mediums, these people born with extraordinary powers, we can communicate with the souls of the departed dead—perhaps our own loved ones, perhaps somebody else, unknown to us, who has passed on but is still interested in this world and ready to help it.

These departed spirits are supposed to come to us and help us in different ways. You have read about table rappings and messages given, perhaps, when a man lets a pen rest upon his fingers and allows it to move, seemingly by itself. You may also have read of the messages people claim to have received from mediums.

What is the value of this contact with the dead? Well, we are told that it gives us information about the state of the beloved, about their condition, what is happening to them, how they are living: life in the unseen realm. It also gives us facts about ourselves. We are helped to know our own future. We are warned against certain dangers, and given advice about our problems.

Some spiritists even claim to heal diseases. One spiritist says that he is controlled, if I remember rightly, by the departed spirit of the great Louis Pasteur, the man who started the science of bacteriology; the first discoverer of germs. He claims that the departed spirit of Louis Pasteur enables him to diagnose illnesses and heal patients.

Finally, as we have seen, spiritists say that it is even possible for departed spirits to materialise before us. A kind of astral body is formed round the spirit so that we actually see and recognise our loved one. This is why this teaching is so subtle. It is claimed that such materialisations must be an absolute proof of the truth of spiritism, because you are seeing the very person you are longing to see.

The danger of spiritism
Now all this is denounced in the Scriptures from beginning to end, but it is not enough just to say that. God willing, I hope to go on in my next study to give you the scriptural answer to this teaching, and to produce the reasons why, as Christian people, we should not only not touch this kind of thing but should also be aware of its danger and be forearmed against it.

'We wrestle not against flesh and blood, but against principalities, against powers, against the rulers of the darkness of this world, against spiritual wickedness in high places.' Is the world going back to this kind of bondage? There are evidences that it is, and that in all its devilish subtlety spiritism is trying to insinuate itself even into the Christian Church.

It is a lie to say that the resurrection of Christ was a spirit appearance. That is not what is taught in the Scriptures. Any so-called materialisation is a counterfeit of the devil and of these powers, these forces. So you see why it is important for us to know something about this subject?

You may feel that this study has been a sheer waste of time. Ah yes, you are well at the moment and your loved ones are with you and everything is all right. But wait until your little world is suddenly shattered by illness, or you are bereaved and brokenhearted and desperate. Then what will you do if somebody comes along and says, 'I'm a Christian like you. I can give you great comfort. You needn't bear this burden alone'?

It is when they are ignorant that Christian people become the dupes of spiritist teaching. If you do not know about these things and about how the devil and his followers can transform themselves into angels of light, they will be able to ensnare you—'the snare of the devil', Paul calls it in 2 Timothy 2:26—and you will become a victim and a captive, and it can lead to terrible results.

We must know about these matters and consider them, in order that we may see that we must be 'strong in the Lord, and in the power of His might', because safety lies only in putting on 'the whole armour of God' Himself.

3

SPIRITISM
AND
THE CHRISTIAN

'Finally, my brethren, be strong in the Lord, and in the power of his might. Put on the whole armour of God, that ye may be able to stand against the wiles of the devil. For we wrestle not against flesh and blood, but against principalities, against powers, against the rulers of the darkness of this world, against spiritual wickedness in high places.Wherefore take unto you the whole armour of God, that ye may be able to withstand in the evil day, and having done all, to stand.' (Eph. 6:10-13)

We come now in our consideration of demonology to what is most important from our Christian standpoint. The apostle tells us that we must wrestle against this wrong teaching and must learn how to stand against it. And our business now is to discover how we do that. In other words, what is the answer given by the teaching of the Bible and the Christian gospel to the claims put forward in the name of spiritism?

THE FACTS OF SPIRITISM

Now it seems to me that the best approach is something like this.

Facing the facts

First of all, we do not deny the facts and the phenomena in toto. Now I say 'in toto' because we know that many frauds have been exposed. I have referred to the Society for Psychical Research, which, throughout the years, has investigated many of the claims that have been put forward and has been able to prove very satisfactorily that <u>many were bogus</u>. But—and this is the point I am emphasising—they <u>are not all fraudulent.</u> In spite of the most careful investigations undertaken by people who are not spiritists, the Society has had to admit that it has been left with certain phenomena which cannot be explained.

Healings have taken place, and it is no use disputing them: they are facts, and it is never a part of Christianity to deny facts. You do not strengthen the Christian case by simply dismissing something—I am referring to facts, not theories—it is not only not scientific to deny facts, it is not Christian. Christianity faces facts and does not care where they come from, whether from science or some other source. We must never base our position upon obscurantism, upon a refusal to face well-attested facts.

The Bible itself grants that phenomena may very well be produced. Take, for instance, our Lord's own statement in <u>Matthew 24:24:</u> 'For there shall arise false Christs, and false prophets, and shall shew great signs and wonders; insomuch that, if it were possible, they shall deceive the very elect.' Now that is a very strong statement. Our Lord warns us that these lying spirits will be able to perform such amazing wonders that even the very elect of God may be tempted to believe.

And, of course, going back to the Old Testament, the magicians of Egypt were able to reproduce, up to a point, the things that were done by Moses. Paul reminds Timothy that Jannes and Jambres withstood Moses and says that he must not be surprised at such opposition and such manifestations in his own time (2 Tim. 3:8). Extraordinary things can and do happen.

Learning from the facts

Having accepted the facts, we must then ask: What is their value? Here again, it is important to be clear in our thinking. Is there any value in these facts?

Now I suggest that, up to a point, they have a very real value in that they are undoubtedly a proof of the reality of the spiritual realm. They demonstrate that there are unseen powers that are able to do marvellous things, that are able to influence people, able to influence the body, able to produce phenomena, even able to have an effect upon inanimate objects. Up to that point they demonstrate the reality of these principalities and powers, 'the rulers of the darkness of this world', the 'spiritual wickedness in high places'.

But let us be careful! True Christians already believe in that realm; they believe in the testimony of the Scripture, so they do not need the proofs. But although they do not need them, they can recognise them. Look at it like this: until comparatively recently, in most civilised countries the prevailing and controlling view of the whole of life was the purely materialistic view that had become popular towards the end of the nineteenth century and persisted into the twentieth century. We did not believe in a spiritual realm at all. Everything was material, and everything could be explained in material terms. The atom was the ultimate piece of matter and there was nothing smaller. There it was: it was solid. And the whole of the spiritual realm was entirely excluded.

Now the facts and phenomena produced by spiritism were of great value in countering such a materialistic view. I am not saying that what they taught us was right, but at any rate they were saying that there was a spiritual realm, there was another realm that we could not see but that was there and could influence this realm. This is, of course, not so necessary today because that old materialism has gone. Scientists have found that their atom is a hive of very great activity and power, and now they are spiritualising almost everything. Everything is force and movement and energy.

Explaining the facts

Now here we come to the dividing line. We have accepted the facts. As Christians, we have seen that we can agree with spiritists in saying that there is a spiritual realm, and that there are powers and forces beyond us, beyond our understanding, that are able to influence life in this world.

But how are they to be explained? This is where we, as Christians, become most concerned. And the answer seems to me to be something like this: we start with the great fact of the biblical condemnation of spiritism. The Bible has no reservations: it condemns spiritism in its entirety. We read in 1 Samuel, 'Now Samuel was dead, and all Israel had lamented him, and buried him in Ramah, even in his own city. And Saul had put away those that had familiar spirits, and the wizards, out of the land' (1 Sam. 28:3).

Here was the first king of Israel, Saul, called of God and anointed, and that was one of his first actions. We are told again about this ban in the ninth verse of this chapter: 'And the woman [the so-called witch of Endor] said unto him, Behold, thou knowest what Saul hath done, how he hath cut off those that have familiar spirits, and the wizards, out of the land; wherefore then layest thou a snare for my life, to cause me to die?'

But there is another example that is, perhaps, still more interesting. Later on there was a very good king, Josiah, who reigned after an evil time in the history of this people of Israel, and who was suddenly awakened to the evil of the times. He began to take action, and a reformation followed. There was a kind of revival in the days of Josiah, one of the notable revivals in the story of the children of Israel. You will find the account of it in 2 Kings 23:24:

> Moreover the workers with familiar spirits, and the wizards, and the images, and the idols, and all the abominations that were spied in the land of Judah

and in Jerusalem, did Josiah put away, that he might perform the words of the law which were written in the book that Hilkiah the priest found in the house of the Lord.

The account goes on to say this about Josiah:

And like unto him was there no king before him, that turned to the LORD with all his heart, and with all his soul, and with all his might, according to all the law of Moses; neither after him arose there any like him.

So here is an exceptional king, and you see what he does: he clears out all those 'workers with familiar spirits', the spiritists, the mediums, referred to here as 'abominations', that were defiling the land of Israel. That is, therefore, a very notable testimony.

But consider also the verdict on Saul in 1 Chronicles 10:13-14:

So Saul died for his transgression which he committed against the LORD, even against the word of the LORD, which he kept not, and also for asking counsel of one that had a familiar spirit, to enquire of it; and enquired not of the LORD.

That was why Saul died as he did. He died for his transgression, and part of his downfall and his condemnation was that he consulted the woman of Endor, who was able to manipulate a familiar spirit.

Then we find a very striking condemnation of spiritism in the book of the prophet Isaiah, chapter 8, verses 19 and 20:

> And when they shall say unto you, Seek unto them
> that have familiar spirits, and unto wizards that peep,
> and that mutter: should not a people seek unto their
> God? for the living to the dead? To the law and to the
> testimony: if they speak not according to this word, it
> is because there is no light in them.

Now there is the great prophet Isaiah, commissioned
by God and given a revelation and a teaching, and he
prohibits and ridicules the very notion of turning to
familiar spirits. 'For the living', he says, 'to the dead?'
Such thing is monstrous. And so he condemns it root
and branch.

Every time there was a new move towards God in the
life of Israel, anything in the direction of a reformation
and revival, spiritism was excluded; witches and
mediums were only sought out by desperate people, like
Saul, after they had gone astray. We deduce, therefore,
that according to biblical teaching, consulting spiritists
is clearly evil. And it is not only evil, it is degrading.
They 'peep', they 'mutter'. There is something ugly and
unclean about spiritism; it is an abomination. Trying
to get a message from the dead, going to a medium or
to a meeting where you can get this kind of help for
your health or for any other reason, is foul.

The Christian's response
Of course, for Christian people such a prohibition
ought to be enough in and of itself. When something is
condemned as plainly and as explicitly as spiritism is
in the Scriptures, a Christian should not even desire to
know about it, still less consult it. And in addition, the

fact that this practice was rampant among the pagan races who dwelt in darkness should also be sufficient to deter the Christian.

WHY IS SPIRITISM CONDEMNED?

But let us go further. Why do you think the Bible should be so strong and so clear in its denunciation of all forms of spiritism? It seems to me that, in the light of the biblical passages we have just read, we can arrive at the following answers in terms of principles.

God's revelation

The attempt to consult spirits is wrong because it sets revelation completely on one side: by which I mean the Bible itself. Take the way the prophet Isaiah puts it in chapter 8: 'To the law and to the testimony' (v. 20). That is God's way. The same point is made in the denunciation of Saul in 1 Chronicles 10 where we are told that Saul was asking counsel of one that had a familiar spirit and 'enquired not of the LORD' (v. 14).

No, we are to be a people who 'seek unto their God'. 'For the living to the dead?' No! 'To the law and to the testimony'. Spiritism puts the whole of the biblical revelation on one side. In the Bible we are given the teaching that is necessary for the soul in every respect. That is the business of the Bible: to teach us the truth about God and ourselves; how to live, how to die, the world, and the life beyond. God has given it for our instruction. But in spiritism we see a teaching which says that this is not enough and is of no value. Spiritists must seek some life and some knowledge and information elsewhere. The Bible is not good enough for them; They must take this other, this prohibited action. I emphasise again that in and of itself that is enough to condemn spiritism. Anything that puts God's gracious revelation entirely on one side is self-condemning.

Christian doctrine

Spiritism not only sets the whole of revelation on one side, it denies specific teaching within the revelation. It is wrong in principle and it is wrong in practice, in the details.

Angels

Take, for instance the teaching in the Scriptures about good angels and bad angels and about the principalities and powers. Spiritism is only interested in the spirits of the departed dead and explains angels in terms of the activity of departed spirits. It does not recognise the biblical teaching concerning these great spiritual powers and forces, and that, in itself, is very serious.

Teaching about our Lord

But still more serious is the attitude of spiritists to our blessed Lord Himself. That is where spiritism becomes absolutely impossible for a Christian. As I have already indicated, spiritists maintain that our Lord was just an outstanding genius in His sensitivity to the spiritual realm. He was the supreme medium; the almost perfect, if not the perfect, medium. And so it is claimed that His miracles of healing were but the works of one who was in close contact with the unseen spirit realm. He was so sensitive and so much in control, that he was able to exercise the functions of a medium. It is said that there are 'spiritualist healers' today. We read about them in the papers, and see how they claim to heal people in large numbers, and so on. Well, we are told that our Lord did that to a still greater extent. And so his miracles are not explained, as the Bible explains them, as signs of his deity and of his unique belonging to the Godhead. It is all brought down to a human level.

Now in John's Gospel, the Greek word used for miracle is a word meaning 'sign': 'This beginning of signs did Jesus in Cana of Galilee' (John 2:11). Our Lord himself taught that his miracles were signs. He said to the people one day, 'Though ye believe not me, believe the works' (John 10:38). In effect, he said, 'You keep on asking me who I am and you do not believe in me. Well, if you do not believe my words, why not believe my works? Look at what I am doing. These works prove who I am.'

And when John the Baptist was in trouble and sent two of his disciples to ask our Lord, 'Art thou he that should come, or do we look for another?' (Matt. 11:3), the answer was: 'Go and shew John again those things which ye do hear and see: the blind receive their sight, and the lame walk, the lepers are cleansed, and the deaf hear, the dead are raised up' (Matt. 11:4-5). John was to consider the significance of that. The miracles were attestations of the fact that our Lord was the Son of God.

The resurrection

And, of course, it is the same exactly with our Lord's resurrection. I have pointed out to you that according to the teaching of spiritism, our Lord's resurrection falls into the category of the materialisation of spirits. It is claimed that some mediums have power to cause the materialisation, as it were, of spirits, so that spirits of the departed dead appear in some form—not real, but some kind of appearance.

But our Lord himself has dealt with this. In the last chapter of Luke's Gospel, we are told that the disciples were in the upper room with the doors shut because they were afraid of the Jews. And then we read:

> As they thus spake, Jesus himself stood in the midst of them, and saith unto them, Peace be unto you. But they were terrified and affrighted, and supposed that they had seen a spirit. And he said unto them, Why are ye troubled? and why do thoughts arise in your hearts? Behold my hands and my feet, that it is I myself: handle me, and see; for a spirit hath not flesh and bones, as ye see me have. And when he had thus spoken, he shewed them his hands and his feet' (Luke 24:36-40).

Now there is our Lord's specific denial of the very things that spiritists say about him. He says: I am not a spirit. I am not a ghost. Look at me. Handle me. See, it is I myself.

Spiritists rob the resurrection of its uniqueness and of its supreme glory. Our Lord literally rose in the body. This was not the 'appearance' of a spirit. The body was glorified. It was changed, but it was still essentially the same body. It was not the materialisation of his spirit only. That is a lie, a denial of the resurrection. And, as the apostle Paul says, 'If Christ be not risen [from the dead], then is our preaching vain, and your faith is also vain ... ye are yet in your sins ... we are of all men most miserable' (1 Cor. 15:14, 17, 19).

The way of salvation

How is the world to be evangelised? How are men and women to be brought to live the right life? The teaching of this cult is that all people should know that we can be in contact with this other realm, and get help from it. That is the way to conquer the problems of life, that is the way of salvation. Of course, that was exactly what the rich man, Dives, believed in our Lord's parable about Dives and Lazarus. There is Dives in hell and this is what he says to Abraham:

> I pray thee therefore, father, that thou wouldest send him [Lazarus] to my father's house: for I have five brethren; that he may testify unto them, lest they also come into this place of torment. Abraham saith unto him, They have Moses and the prophets; let them hear them. And he said, Nay, father Abraham: but if one went unto them from the dead, they will repent. And he said unto him, If they hear not Moses and the prophets, neither will they be persuaded, though one rose from the dead (Luke 16:27-31).

You see the argument? Dives thinks that if only a spirit would appear from the other realm and tell people, then they would believe and be helped.

No, no, says Abraham, that is not God's way. They have Moses and the prophets. That is God's way.

Spiritism offers another way of salvation. It says that what God has provided is inadequate. It is a denial of God's great and wonderful salvation.

God's final judgment

Spiritism totally denies the biblical teaching with regard to hell, eternal punishment, and God's retribution upon the ungodly. Spiritists will tell you that the future realm is very much like this one; men and women still go on doing very much the same things, drinking their whiskies, smoking, playing cards. There is no heaven and hell, but the future life is just a continuation of this life. So they say, 'Don't be frightened of death. It's all right, your life continues, but it's much nicer there, it's much better and much happier.' And poor, lost, benighted, bemused souls believe this teaching.

But the biblical doctrine says that there is a great division: heaven and hell; to be with God in glory, or suffering and everlasting destruction. There is nothing that is right about spiritist teaching. It is altogether opposed to God and to everything that he has done for humanity in his infinite grace and kindness and compassion. It lulls people into a false sense of security and of peace, and robs them of a true concern about their souls and their final salvation.

Evil spirits

Let me give you a third reason why spiritism must be condemned. People think they are talking to their own departed dead, but they are not. According to the Bible, they are communicating with evil spirits that are impersonating their loved ones. These evil spirits have very great power and knowledge and they can, as it were, materialise themselves. 'Look here,' says Paul, in effect, in Ephesians 6, 'you are not up against flesh and blood. You are up against terrible forces who are great in knowledge and understanding and power. They know the facts, and therefore they can impersonate others with the object of deluding poor benighted souls.'

But here I imagine somebody putting an objection to me. The spiritists certainly will. They say, 'You are making a sweeping statement and saying that evil spirits are impersonating the departed dead. But what about when Saul consulted the woman of Endor? The Bible says that Samuel himself actually appeared. Isn't this the whole case for spiritism? Saul went to see the woman and when she asked Saul who he would like to consult, he said, "Samuel." And so she, as a medium, was able to call up Samuel. Is that not an absolute proof of spiritism?'

But the answer, of course, is that that particular case is one of the strongest denunciations of spiritism to be found anywhere in the Bible. Does the record not make it abundantly clear that the woman of Endor did not call up Samuel but that Samuel came in spite of her? Listen to the account: 'Then said the woman, Whom shall I bring up unto thee? And he said, Bring me up Samuel'—and this is immediately followed by—'And when the woman saw Samuel, she cried with

68

a loud voice: and the woman spake to Saul saying, Why hast thou deceived me? for thou art Saul. And the king said unto her, Be not afraid ... ' (1 Sam. 28:11-13).

Now there is only one explanation of that. No doubt the woman was on the point of trying, as she thought, to call up Samuel, but before she had a chance to do anything, Samuel appeared. Why was the woman so alarmed and amazed? Because she had done nothing! Samuel suddenly appeared and she was filled with terror. She 'cried with a loud voice'. She lost control of herself. Normally when she did this kind of thing she was in control of the situation. She was not frightened and did not cry out. But she had never seen anything like this before.

And then, in addition to that, we have Samuel's condemnation of Saul's action. God was correcting and punishing King Saul for attempting to consult Samuel. In this incident, something quite exceptional happened. God gave this appearance of Samuel in order to condemn a practice he had already condemned through Saul himself. So, far from being a case of the exercise of spiritist power, we see a medium overwhelmed and terrified because of the action of God himself in condemnation of the trade that she was following.

Then there is the case of the transfiguration of Jesus. People may say, 'But surely on the Mount of Transfiguration Moses and Elijah appeared and spoke to our Lord, and the disciples recognised them.'

That, of course, is perfectly true.

'Well, then,' asks somebody, 'doesn't that substantiate the case for spiritism?'

But the answer is that there was no spiritualistic procedure at all. Our Lord did not stand there and say, 'Now I'm going to call up Moses and Elijah.' Quite the contrary. We are told that they 'appeared'. This, of course, was a unique event in our Lord's earthly life. First he, himself, was transfigured before his disciples. Then Moses and Elijah came. Why? As the representatives of the law and the prophets. And what were Moses and Elijah doing? We are told that they were discussing with our Lord the exodus that he should accomplish at Jerusalem, this great crisis. They were discussing his death with him.

It all suddenly comes together. Here is our Lord, the fulfiller of the law and the prophets, and they are with him, and he is going to do this work. The transfiguration is one of the vital, significant events in connection with our Lord's death and is wonderful teaching for us. It has nothing to do with spiritism at all. Its effect upon the disciples is a further and a final proof of that. The whole place was overshadowed by the glory of God. Nothing could be more different from a seance. It is the exact opposite.

A further reason for saying that spiritism is the work of evil spirits is that you will invariably find that people who hold to spiritism never glorify the Lord Jesus Christ. I am speaking plainly. Look at the people who claim that they belong to Christian churches but are also interested in spiritism. Examine their views on the deity of Christ; ask them about the virgin birth and miracles; find out their ideas on the meaning of our Lord's death and the atonement; ask what they think about the literal, physical resurrection. They never glorify him. Never! This is a significant and interesting fact. It is when people depart from the faith that they begin to believe in this kind of teaching.

Then examine the life of many of these mediums. I have known some of them, one in particular, who became a Christian. And I want to quote a phrase that that woman used. Here was a woman who made her living as a spiritist medium, earning her three guineas almost every Sunday night. One Sunday she was unable, because of a slight illness, to go and do what she normally did. As she was sitting in her house, she saw people walking to a place of worship. Quite suddenly, she thought to herself, 'What if I went with them? I wonder what they do there? I wonder what that place is like in comparison with what we do?' So she went to that place of worship and that led to her conversion. She never again did what she had been doing before.

But I want to quote to you her reply to my question, 'What did you feel like when you came to this service?'

'Well,' she said, 'this was what really convinced me and finally convicted me. When I came into this place, I felt immediately that there was spiritual power here, exactly as we have in our meetings. I was always conscious of power in our meetings and I was conscious of power in your meeting, but there was one great difference. The power in this building here, in some indefinable way, seemed to me to be clean. I didn't think of it. I wasn't reasoning. I was just conscious of power and of cleanliness and of purity such as I've never known before.'

That is it! Spiritism is unclean. You will often find that the people who dabble in it, especially mediums, are immoral and loose in their living. Moreover, they often collapse and have mental breakdowns and various other problems. I repeat that they are not in touch with the spirits of the departed dead, but with evil spirits impersonating the dead.

Faith in God

But, finally, this cult must be condemned because it springs from a lack of trust in God and in his way of salvation.

Now I want to elaborate this in headings only. Why do people rush to a medium or go to a spiritist meeting? Do you know why it is? It is because they are not ready to leave their lives and their destiny in the hands of God. They want to take charge; they want to know. There is a fundamental lack of faith and trust in the goodness of God.

But the Christian speaks like this:

My times are in Thy hand:
My God, I wish them there;
My life, my friends, my soul I leave
Entirely to Thy care.

William Freeman Lloyd

Spiritists do not do that. They ask, 'What's happening to my loved one? What's going to happen? What's going to happen to me?' And this is a denial of God and his goodness.

Another hymn says:

Thy way, not mine, O Lord,
However dark it be!

Horatius Bonar

But as well as having no trust in God's goodness, spiritists have no faith in God's ability to help. They say they want guidance, but does God not offer to guide? Why go 'for the living to the dead'? Isaiah and the writer of 1 Chronicles ask: Why not seek your God? 'To the law and to the testimony'. God offers guidance, but it is not enough for these people. They have to go to familiar spirits. They want wisdom, they want to know what to do. But the Bible says, 'If any of you lack wisdom, let him ask of God, that giveth to all men liberally, and upbraideth not' (James 1:5). All the wisdom you can ever need, God offers to give it all.

Health? It is the same. 'I am the LORD that healeth thee' (Exod. 15:26). That was one of the names God gave himself when he spoke to the children of Israel of old. You desire comfort? Ah, that is why people go to these spiritist mediums. They go there for comfort because they know nothing about the glorious comfort and consolation that is given here, in the Scriptures, and by the Spirit who has been sent to be our Comforter—that is his name!

The future life? Spiritists consult the dead, but that is not the way the apostle Paul looked to the future, was it? What is death? Ah, said Paul, 'To be with Christ; which is far better' (Phil. 1:23). That was Paul's way. Do you want to know the future? Well, read your Bible, and learn about the blessed hope that awaits you: the coming of Christ; 'new heavens and a new earth, wherein dwelleth righteousness' (2 Pet. 3:13); your very body glorified like his glorious body. We shall see him as he is and be like him. What more do you want? But these people, they brush it all aside and consult the dead about the living.

Can you not see that spiritism is a denial of everything that we hold dear? It is a denial of the Father and the Son and the Holy Spirit. It is a denial of the Father's providential care and of his love.

'But,' people say, 'I don't know what to do; I don't know where to turn.'

Listen, my friend, 'The very hairs of your head are all numbered' (Matt. 10:30). Is that not enough for you? What more do you need? God, your heavenly Father, in his providential care, knows all about you. Nothing can happen to you apart from him. If he cares for the lilies of the field and the birds of the air, how much more for you? That is our Lord's teaching.

Spiritism is a denial of the sufficiency and the grace of the indwelling Son, our blessed Lord and Saviour. I want strength. I want guidance. I want healing. I want comfort. Listen, says Paul, 'I have learned, in whatsoever state I am, therewith to be content. I know both how to be abased, and I know how to abound ... I can do all things through Christ which strengtheneth me' (Phil. 4:11-13). Yes, says Charles Wesley:

Thou, O Christ, art all I want!
More than all in Thee I find.

These people know nothing about that. They deny the Son. He is all-sufficient, but they consult familiar spirits. Oh, the tragedy! Listen to these glorious words of Wesley:

> Thou hidden source of calm repose,
> Thou all-sufficient love divine,
> My help and refuge from my foes,
> Secure I am, if Thou art mine:
> And lo! From sin, and grief, and shame,
> I hide me, Jesus, in Thy Name.
>
> Jesus, my all in all Thou art,
> My rest in toil, my ease in pain,
> The medicine of my broken heart,
> In war, my peace; in loss, my gain;
> My smile beneath the tyrant's frown;
> In shame my glory and my crown.
>
> In want, my plentiful supply;
> In weakness, mine almighty power;
> In bonds, my perfect liberty,
> My light in Satan's darkest hour;
> My help and stay whene'er I call;
> My life in death, my heaven, my all.

And spiritists deny the Holy Spirit. They know nothing about his communion. They do not say, 'The grace of the Lord Jesus Christ, and the love of God, and the fellowship and the communion of the Holy Spirit.' They do not know anything about the guide and the comforter whom our Lord said he was going to send. He said, 'I will not leave you comfortless' (John 14:18). He says, in effect, 'I will not leave you orphans. Do not be alarmed because I say I am going. Let not your heart be troubled. I am going to send you another comforter, someone who will always be with you. He will be in you and he will never leave you.'

The Christian who turns to spiritism is either displaying his total unbelief or his total ignorance. He is so uninstructed that he knows nothing of the exceeding riches of God's grace, the unsearchable riches of Christ and the comfort and consolation of the Holy Spirit.

CHRISTIAN RESISTANCE

No, no, my friends, resist this false teaching, 'stedfast in the faith' (1 Pet. 5:9). This is the work of the 'principalities' and 'powers', 'the rulers of the darkness of this world', of 'spiritual wickedness in high places'. This is one of the masterpieces of the devil, who is always trying to counterfeit both the Scriptures, and, above all, the Son of God.

Put on the whole armour of God. 'Be strong in the Lord and in the power of his might ... that ye may be able to withstand in the evil day, and having done all, to stand.'

4

DEVIL POSSESSION

'Finally, my brethren, be strong in the Lord, and in the power of his might. Put on the whole armour of God, that ye may be able to stand against the wiles of the devil. For we wrestle not against flesh and blood, but against principalities, against powers, against the rulers of the darkness of this world, against spiritual wickedness in high places. Wherefore take unto you the whole armour of God, that ye may be able to withstand in the evil day, and having done all, to stand.' (Eph. 6:10-13)

We come now to consider involuntary submission to the power of these evil forces by which we are surrounded. The last subject, spiritism, was a kind of voluntary submission—people seeking knowledge and comfort and power from evil spirits. But now we will look at those people who do not submit voluntarily but find themselves subjected to the influence of these terrible and terrifying powers. This is what is commonly known as devil possession.

WHAT IS DEVIL POSSESSION?

Now first we must try to be clear in our minds as to what this means, and I think that the term is a very good one. It means that the person is actually being possessed by, or controlled by, somebody else, something else, some other power. For the time being someone is owned, as it were, by this other person, guided by this other power, this spirit, controlled by it. The person is no longer in control of himself or herself, but has been mastered, taken over, by an unseen spiritual power.

Changed behaviour

When we come to manifestations, therefore, we shall find that one of the most characteristic is that the personality of this person who is devil-possessed seems temporarily to have been entirely changed. The result is that the poor possessed person begins to act in a strange, unusual manner, is no longer able to function as he normally does, or is at times deprived of the normal use of his faculties. In other words, in the accounts of this condition, we find that violence is at times manifested.

Take the case of the so-called man of Gadara—the violence, the way he cut himself with stones and dwelt among the tombs (Mark 5:1-5). All that is evidence of the abnormal behaviour to which I am referring. And then there is the boy whom our Lord found with his father at the foot of the Mount of Transfiguration. We read that he was frequently thrown into the fire and burned, or thrown into water, and so on (Matt. 17:14-18). In Luke 11, we read of a man with a 'dumb spirit' who could not speak. There is sometimes deafness, and sometimes blindness. These are the various ways in which the spirit manifests himself and his control through the poor possessed person.

Unusual knowledge

Another feature which, to me, is a very notable and important aspect of the whole subject is that clearly these spirits are able to give people unusual knowledge and information. In the New Testament it is striking to observe how these devil-possessed persons were able to recognise our Lord. The Pharisees and scribes and Sadducees did not, but these possessed people did. When they saw him, they made their statements: 'Thou art the Christ the Son of God' (Luke 4:41); 'Thou art the Son of God' (Mark 3:11); 'Jesus, thou Son of the Most High God' (Mark 5:7), and so on. And the girl with a 'spirit of divination' had the power and insight to recognise the unusual quality of Paul and Silas. She said, 'These men are the servants of the most high God, which shew unto us the way of salvation' (Acts 16:17). Sometimes an ignorant, illiterate person is found speaking in almost perfect Greek or Latin, or in some other language, which such a person has not only never learned but could probably not learn. Under this influence they are given a knowledge and a power and a capacity entirely above their level.

WHY LEARN ABOUT DEVIL POSSESSION?

Is there anybody, I wonder, who feels that we are wasting our time, that this is a remote and theoretical subject that has nothing to say to us and to our experience? If there is such person, let me give you some reasons why it is very important for us to consider this subject.

The whole revelation of God

One reason, of course, which is sufficient in and of itself, is that this subject is a part of the exposition of the verses we are looking at. The apostle Paul felt that it was so important that he put it here, at the very end of his epistle, and he puts it with great emphasis. Anything that is in the Scriptures is important for us. If you feel that any part of the Scriptures has nothing to say to you, then there is something seriously wrong with you. If you pick and choose in the Scriptures and only read your favourite passages because you think they will help you, then you are a babe, an infant! Indeed, one might even query whether you are born at all. The Scripture—the whole of the Scripture—is for us, and we are to know it and to study it and to understand it as best we can.

The background to the Bible

But let me go beyond that. I venture to suggest that nobody can really read the Bible – the four Gospels particularly – in an intelligent manner who does not know something about this vital subject. It is one of the most frightening and prominent features of the earthly life and ministry of our blessed Lord and Saviour. And it is not only in the Gospels; demon possession appears in the Old Testament—we have looked at one illustration, and there are others. It is also to be found in the book of Acts.

I repeat that without knowledge of this subject you really cannot understand the background to the Bible and the real meaning of many of the scriptures.

Secular and Church history

But in addition to that, if you have ever troubled to read the history of this country or of any other European country, you will have found that devil possession had great prominence in the Middle Ages and was a very real problem at that time. If you take an intelligent interest in history, and especially in the history of the Church, you are bound to know something about this because some of the most terrible abuses of the Roman Catholic Church in the Middle Ages came in directly as the result of devil possession.

The work of missionaries

But, to be more up to date, devil possession is a problem in many places in the world today where people are in a backward, primitive condition and are still under the domination of paganism. So if you are interested in missionary work, or are proposing to be a missionary yourself, or if you are trying to pray intelligently for your friends who are missionaries, then the more you know about this subject, the more you will be able to help them.

The danger posed by spiritism

But nearer home, as we have seen, there is a new interest in spiritism in this country, and spiritism is even entering the Church. This adds urgency to our study of demon possession because it is quite clear to me that many of the so-called mediums become devil possessed. Having submitted themselves voluntarily to these other powers, they frequently get into a state in which they cannot keep themselves from them, and they become subject to them and possessed by them. That is one of the most dangerous aspects of spiritism as a whole.

Teaching about self-abandonment

Then another reason is that certain types of Christianity, and some cults, teach people to abandon themselves and their own self-control. Indeed, people are deliberately worked up into a kind of excitement in which they lose themselves. And it seems to me that that kind of teaching opens the door directly to devil possession. The moment you surrender your understanding and discrimination, and abandon yourself and your higher controls, you are at the very least putting yourself in a very dangerous position.

Our Lord's words and deeds

But if we need another reason, my next would be sufficient in and of itself. The whole question of our Lord's person is involved here because, as I said, you cannot read the four Gospels without seeing the prominence of devil possession. Our Lord was constantly dealing with devil-possessed people. He exorcised devils, and he sent his disciples out with the power to preach and to cast out devils.

Now, of course, many people reading this face an immediate problem. They do not believe in devils or in angels. They do not really believe in the Holy Spirit. So, they are in difficulties about our Lord because he evidently did believe in these evil spirits and in devil possession.

'Well,' these people say, 'it's quite simple. He was, after all, just a child of his age. He was really only a man and he suffered from the limitations of knowledge that were characteristic of that time. We, of course, in the twentieth century, know so much more. In those days, everybody was concerned with devil possession, and so was he. Like everybody else, he wrongly believed in devils and evil spirits.' This idea that our Lord was mistaken is often taught, and taught in the name of Christ and in the name of the Church.

Other people do not venture to go as far as that but say that, of course, since our Lord was God, as well as man, he did know that devils do not exist, but he accommodated himself to the ignorance of the people. It was not a part of his purpose to enlighten them or correct them or teach them about this subject. He allowed them to go on believing something that was not true. He dealt with these cases as a modern psychologist does, though his technique was slightly different in that he allowed people to believe that he really did have authority to drive out devils. In other words, this 'accommodation theory' maintains that

our Lord deliberately allowed people to believe a lie
and almost encouraged them to do so. He was a great
psychologist, who anticipated much of what is known
and done at the present time.

Again, this teaching is found in books written by
people who claim to be Christians, and some are even
ministers in the Christian Church.

So I repeat that our view of devil possession cannot
be separated from the whole question of the person of
the Lord Jesus Christ, who he was and what he was
doing. That brings me to the next question.

WHY BELIEVE IN DEVIL POSSESSION?

I have been reminding you that there are many people
today – in fact, the vast majority – in the Church, as
well as outside, who do not believe in this at all.

Now there are people who do not believe in God.
There are people who do not believe in angels, in the
Holy Spirit, or, indeed, in the spiritual realm at all.
And, of course, it is perfectly logical and consistent
that such people should not believe in evil spirits. We
shall not waste our time talking about devil possession
with people like that. The problem to discuss with
them is not devil possession but the being of God and
the whole realm of the spiritual.

But there are others – and this is more serious for
us – who, while they do believe in God, in the Lord
Jesus Christ, in the person of the Holy Spirit, and in
the spiritual realm, say that they really cannot believe
in devil possession. They argue that everything which
in the Bible is attributed to devil possession can be very

easily explained in medical terms. 'Surely,' these people say, 'these cases that are described in the Scriptures as devil possession are, most of them, at any rate, simply diseases. In those days, diseases were not understood as they are now. There was a tendency among primitive people to attribute all illness to unseen evil forces and powers, and this is still true of certain benighted people at the present time. 'Therefore,' they add, 'surely now we no longer need to believe in devil possession? It is no denial of the essential faith, and of the teaching of the Scriptures, to say that these were not cases of devil possession but simply straightforward illnesses.'

Now, what is our reply to that? Here are some of the answers.

The testimony of the Scriptures

First and foremost, the Bible itself describes these cases definitely and specifically as devil possession. Nobody can get away from that.

The teaching of our Lord

As I have already said, our Lord himself clearly believed and taught devil possession, so we are again up against the old problem of the authority of the Scriptures. If you take up the position that with the advance of knowledge and the understanding of science you can look down upon the Bible and correct it and show where it is defective, then there is no more to be said. But in that case, we are no longer discussing devil possession, but the authority of the Bible.

If you do accept the authority of the Scriptures, if you believe that the Scriptures are divinely inspired and given by God the Holy Spirit, that the Old Testament prophecies came not from the mind of man, but that 'holy men of God spake as they were moved by the Holy Ghost' (2 Pet. 1:21), and if you believe the same about the authors of the New Testament books— as it seems to me you must, because they claim that for themselves—then you cannot lightly brush aside the reality of devil possession.

The accuracy of the biblical accounts

I have a second argument which seems to me to be even more striking: the Bible is not quite as ignorant as modern men and women tend to believe. Their problem is that they do not know much about the Bible. If they would only read the Bible itself instead of books about the Bible, some of their arguments would immediately have to be abandoned!

Now if the Bible described every form of affliction as devil possession there might be something in the argument of these people. But the Bible itself draws a very sharp distinction between diseases which it recognises as diseases, and devil possession. Let me give you an example. We read in Matthew 4:24: 'And they brought unto him all sick people that were taken with divers diseases and torments, and those which were possessed with devils, and those which were lunatick, and those that had the palsy; and he healed them.' Now that is quite clinical. It would be quite good in a medical text book, would it not? The Bible draws a clear and scientific distinction between diseases, devil possession and lunacy. There is no confusion. The biblical writers were well aware of these different categories.

Let me give you a similar quotation from Luke, who happened to be a doctor himself. This is what he said:

> Now when the sun was setting, all they that had any sick with divers diseases brought them unto him; and he laid his hands on every one of them, and healed them. And devils also came out of many, crying out, and saying, Thou art Christ the Son of God. And he rebuking them suffered them not to speak: for they knew that he was Christ (Luke 4:40-41).

Now there Luke, with his specialist knowledge, draws a sharp distinction between diseases and sickness on the one hand, and devil possession on the other. It is a very significant bit of evidence. This leads me to the next important point.

The symptoms of devil possession

In devil possession there is always *a failure to conform to any known pattern of symptoms for a disease*. This is obviously the basis of the distinction drawn in the two quotations I have just given. That to me is a vital argument.

Here is a man suffering from a disease and he has a complex of symptoms. There is a definite clinical entity or picture. But when you look at a case of devil possession, you see that it can never be put into one or the other of the clinical pictures. That is one of the diagnostic points, one of the ways to differentiate devil possession from a disease.

In addition, there are certain *unusual symptoms which are not found in clinical diseases.* I am referring to the paroxysms and the foaming at the mouth and the violence that we read of in the case of the boy at the foot of the Mount of Transfiguration and violence of the man of Gadara. The boy would throw himself into the fire and water, and the man would cut himself with stones, and so on.

Forgive me, I am going into details because I know that many people are troubled by this. There are those who would not hesitate to say that the boy was obviously an epileptic, to which my reply is that he was very obviously not an epileptic, for the reasons that I have been giving. Epilepsy is a very well recognised clinical entity and I cannot fit this boy into that; there is an additional violence, a going beyond epilepsy, which seems to me to put him into an entirely different category. So we should never refer to him as 'the epileptic boy'.

But we must add that in cases of devil possession, there is also always *the extraordinary element of another personality.* Now when people are sick, their personalities are not changed, not even in cases of lunacy. But here the striking thing is that there is a complete change in the personality. This is a very important point.

Also important is the fact that in the cases of devil possession there is always *a debased element, an element of uncleanness.* You do not see that in disease, but it is always present in devil possession. There is something unhealthy about it all.

The way devil possession is cured

This, again, is a most significant point. The most effective way of bringing about healing is by *prayer*—urgent and intense prayer—for deliverance. And it has often happened. If you are interested in reading about this, read the book about Pastor Hsi of China, which was re-published in an abridged form by the China Inland Mission.[1] Read there about how devil possession was dealt with by Pastor Hsi and his fellow-workers. There are other books that deal with this, but that is one of the best and one of the most popular that I know.

So the work of healing is done by means of prayer but, secondly, there is also *exorcism*, which is the casting out of evil spirits. It may be that this is a subject that we have neglected, not only on the mission field, but, perhaps, in this country of ours as well. Clearly, power to cast out these devils is available to those who are spiritual.

But thirdly, and to me, perhaps most interesting of all, is that sometimes the best way of healing this condition is by the poor devil-possessed person *becoming a Christian.*

Certainly, in my own experience, one of the most striking cases of devil possession I ever saw was healed in this way, and the poor person was entirely delivered.

You say, 'How do you know that this was a case of devil possession?'

1   *Pastor Hsi,* by Geraldine Taylor, is now published by Christian Focus Publications. The China Inland Mission is now the Overseas Missionary Fellowship.

Well, I must not weary you with the details, but I can perfectly illustrate the point I have been making. Here was a poor girl who was supposed to be paralysed, and many doctors had fallen into the trap of thinking that since she could not walk, she had an organic disease, though they could not say which one; none of the doctors could fit the paralysis into any known disease. Then it fell to my lot to see her—partly as a doctor, and partly as a minister—and what struck me immediately was that this was not an organic disease at all, but clearly a case of devil possession. How did I know that? Well, one of the reasons was that when I approached her bed with her doctor and her own minister, the expression on her face changed into something that I will never forget, and though she had not been able to walk for eight years, she began to make the most violent movements with her arms and legs and head, which continued for ten minutes.

But then, as the result of the conversion of two of her sisters, one after another with a good interval between, that poor girl began to attend a place of worship—she was carried there at first—and finally she herself was converted. Nothing was ever said about her paralysis but it just completely disappeared.

Devil possession can happen in Great Britain. These powers and forces are not confined to localities. You must not assume that because a country claims to be educated, this kind of thing cannot take place.

A comparison with other controlled states

'But,' says somebody, 'could what you have been describing not be caused by hallucinations? What about hysteria?'

Differences

My reply is still the same: Devil possession goes beyond either hallucinations or hysteria. The extraordinary knowledge that is given to devil-possessed people—an ignorant girl's ability to speak Latin, for example—cannot be explained in those terms. There is something extra here.

And then, of course, the final argument is surely that if you can explain devil possession in terms of mental states and conditions, hallucinations or hysteria, then what do you make of the case of the Gadarene swine? What happened to them? Can you transfer hysteria to swine?

'Ah,' you say, 'but I don't believe that story.'

Very well! We come back to the point that the problem you are discussing is not demon possession, but your failure to believe the Scriptures. This is a different subject. If you say you believe the Gospel records, but then add, 'I believe this and don't believe that,' then you are not believing in the Gospels but in your own understanding. And how do you know what to believe about the Lord Jesus Christ himself since all you have is what you are told in these Gospels? The Gospels are all careful to tell us that the devils were driven out of the man into the swine which then ran madly and violently over a precipice and were drowned in the sea, about two thousand of them.

Similarities

But let me turn to a positive point. Surely today, in many ways, it ought to be easier to believe in demon possession than at times in the past. Take the practice of hypnotism. It is coming back again, is it not? Now in hypnotism, the hypnotised person is entirely subject to the hypnotist, who takes possession. He can give commands to people who are under his influence and they will obey. He will say, 'Get up!' or 'Sit down!' or 'Sing!'and hypnotised people will do what he says, even though they do not wish to and have not voluntarily decided to. In hypnotism one personality governs and controls another.

Mesmerism is a similar sort of state, only people do not lose consciousness, as it were. But mesmerism is a definite fact. One of the most extraordinary instances that I have ever read was the case of a man called Henry Drummond, one of the converts of D. L. Moody. He who used to travel about a lot with D. L. Moody and was very popular in the Christian Church at the end of the last century.

In the biography of Drummond by George Adam Smith, we read that Drummond could mesmerise people. Before his conversion, when he was a student, he made use of this power to entertain people. He could not only influence a man in his presence, but someone who might be fifty miles away. After his conversion, this became a terrible problem to Drummond because he realised that often, when speaking in meetings, he was mesmerising people, and they were not responding to the gospel at all, but only to him. He had to struggle in order to deal with this and get rid of it.

You see the importance of all this? We are aware today of the fact that one personality can command and control and direct another. It might be argued that this was the explanation of Hitler's rise to power. I myself am quite ready to go further and say that Hitler may very well have been a devil-possessed man. Apparently, he used to go into violent paroxysms. But at the very least, was he not, perhaps, someone with a hypnotic, mesmeric power?

There are other people, also, and I would seriously suggest that this is something that should be borne in mind in mass evangelistic campaigns. Some men who have been much extolled have this capacity and power. You can see it when the Pope makes a public appearance—I have witnessed it in Rome. My point is that it has been clearly demonstrated that it is possible for one human personality to be entirely subjugated to another, without willing or desiring it, and thus become the instrument of another.

The Holy Spirit

Set that against what we are told in the Scriptures about the influence of angels, and, still more, the influence and the power of the Holy Spirit. 'Be not drunk with wine,' says Paul, 'wherein is excess; but be filled with the Spirit' (Eph. 5:18). Submit yourself to the Spirit: let him lead you and guide you and control you. And he does.

The inevitable logical deduction is that if this happens in the realm of the Holy Spirit and of the good angels, the servants of God, why should it not happen in the case of evil spirits, evil angels, and the devil himself? That is where the teaching that we are studying in Ephesians is so important. There are such 'principalities' and 'powers'; there are these 'rulers of the darkness of this world'; there are 'spiritual forces' in these high places; and they can exercise this power. At all costs, says the apostle, remember this so that you may stand against them.

If you believe in the Holy Spirit you must logically believe in these evil spirits. They are there; that is why we call him, *holy* Spirit. Yes, and these powers and forces can indeed dominate a person, and use him and rule over him and manipulate him, even as we are told in such extraordinary detail in the pages of the four Gospels.

WHEN THE DEVIL ATTACKS

'All right,' says somebody, 'but you still leave me with one difficulty, and that is that there does seem, historically, to have been an extraordinary periodicity in the manifestation of devil possession.'

Times of power and times of weakness

Clearly, in the time of our Lord, devil possession was rampant, so much so that some Jews had become exorcists. That is why our Lord was able to turn the argument back on the people who said that he was casting out devils by the power of Beelzebub. He said, 'If I by Beelzebub cast out devils, by whom do your sons cast them out?' (Luke 11:19). But after the time of our Lord, according to the historical records, devil possession more or less disappeared. Then it came back again in the Middle Ages—the dark Middle Ages—when the Church of Rome was dominating the whole of life. It came back in terrible power at that time.

But then, and here is another interesting fact, there was a kind of recrudescence at the time of the Reformation, and immediately after. You will find that whenever there is a great revival of religion there is generally a recurrence of these phenomena. Whenever there is an unusual activity of the Holy Spirit, we see a manifestation of devil possession.

How do you explain this? Surely it must be obvious. Whenever the Spirit of God is present in unusual power, the devil's kingdom is disturbed. The devil sees the threat. Our Lord said, 'If I with the finger of God cast out devils [and that is what he was doing], no doubt the kingdom of God is come upon you' (Luke 11:20). And it had!

But the evil kingdom was filled with terror. So what did it do? It manifested itself in an unusual activity. The presence of the Son of God created a stir in the realm of darkness, and it rose in self-defence in an attempt to defeat him. That is the background to the four Gospels, and it is most important for us to understand this and see its significance.

But we always find that as the result of such a revival, these evil powers are kept in abeyance, and as Christian teaching spreads, they almost entirely disappear. This is not only true of specifically Christian teaching; as long as secular teaching is based upon Christian teaching, and is moral and good and clean and uplifting, then even education and civilisation seem to be able to control these evil powers. That was how the Jewish exorcists were controlling the powers of evil; they were not Christians but they were believers in God, and that alone enabled them.

Now let us be clear about this: there is obviously a great variety in these evil spirits. Some are weak, some are strong; some are vile, some are terribly vile. You notice how our Lord puts it: a spirit that is driven out brings back with it seven other spirits even worse than itself (Matt. 12:45). So there are gradations. Some of these spirits seem to be very weak. I would not hesitate to assert that in one instance I was able myself, by the mere exercise of will power and authority, to quell one such feeble, evil spirit tormenting a poor girl.

The danger today

General education and teaching can keep these powers at bay and it undoubtedly has had this effect during the last hundred years or so. But—and this is what is so important today—in an age of moral declension, in an age of godlessness, in an age of excesses, in an age when people no longer believe in God and begin to dabble with the unseen and to play with evil, invariably this phenomenon comes back. When their education becomes purely secular and denies the Bible entirely and denies God and becomes atheistical, then, though people become sophisticated and have a knowledge of a kind, it is not sufficient to withstand the onslaught of these evil powers. So I am suggesting that in this evil, godless, immoral age in which we are living, which is arrogantly flaunting itself, flouting the sanctities and standing arrogantly against God and almost returning to the position in the eighteenth century when there were devil worshippers here in London, in an age like this, there is the awful and terrible danger of a recurrence of devil possession, especially as spiritism becomes more and more popular.

THE COMING OF THE DELIVERER

What, then, is our conclusion? It is this: thank God for the season of Advent.[2] Thank God that we are in the time of the year when we think of the coming of the Son of God. Oh, the difference his coming has made! He came to deliver us not only from the guilt and punishment of sin, but from the power of evil. He came 'that he might destroy [undo] the works of the devil' (1 John 3:8).

The account in Matthew's Gospel of the healing of the two demon-possessed men has a most interesting and significant statement. Matthew tells us that when the men approached our Lord, the devils realised what was happening. They recognised him; they knew his superior power. They knew he was going to drive them out and they said, 'Art thou come hither to torment us before the time?' (Matt. 8:29). Thank God for that. It means that our Lord, by his coming, has not only dealt with these demonic powers and controlled and quelled them and delivered his people from them, but also that a time is coming when, with the devil at their head, they will finally be altogether destroyed. The principalities and powers, the world rulers of this darkness, the spiritual forces in the heavenly places, and the devil—the prince of them all—will be cast into a lake of everlasting destruction, and will have no more influence and no more power whatsoever.

---

2   These sermons were preached in November/December 1960.

'Art thou come to destroy us before the time?' The time is coming! It is the time of our Lord's glorious return, and you and I who are Christians look forward to that. Thank God that in the meantime we can be 'strong in the Lord, and in the power of his might'; we can 'put on the whole armour of God'. And let us use this liberty, and the knowledge it has brought us, to help others, to warn them, to open their eyes to the terrible dangers which are surrounding them. The time is coming! Amen.

Other titles in this series
by Dr Martyn Lloyd-Jones....

———————

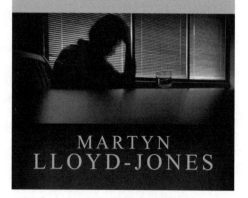

Introduced by Kevin DeYoung

FAITH
ON TRIAL

PSALM 73

MARTYN
LLOYD-JONES

ISBN 978-1-84550-696-4

Faith on Trial

Psalm 73

MARTYN LLOYD-JONES

For anyone who has ever wondered if life is fair, or if God is fair, these sermons will speak to your predicament. The Doctor will apply the balm of Scripture to soothe your soul and strengthen your faith.

Kevin DeYoung, Senior Pastor,
University Reformed Church. East Lansing, Michigan

When this book first appeared in 1965, I was an undergraduate reading chemistry and mathematics. I recall thinking as I read the book that this Lloyd-Jones chap (whom at that point I still had not met) had a God-given ability to meditate on a text, and ponder it within the framework of the entire Bible. I have not changed my mind, but I would now add as well that his exposition of Psalm 73 is saturated with spiritual wisdom designed to help Christians face trials and temptations of many sorts. I am very thankful to God to see this book come back into print.

D. A. Carson, Research Professor of New Testament,
Trinity Evangelical Divinity School, Deerfield, Illinois

Why do good people suffer unjustly – and yet others get away with it? The Psalmist, Asaph, dealt with this very problem in Psalm 73 – one that has often perplexed and discouraged God's people. Asaph reveals his own 'no-holds-barred' feelings and leads us step by step from near-despair to final assurance. For this reason it has always appealed to preachers and counsellors. An excellent book for those struggling with, or wondering about, injustice in the world.

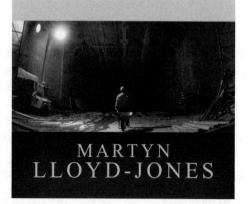

Introduced by Thabiti Anyabwile

OUT OF THE DEPTHS

PSALM 51

MARTYN LLOYD-JONES

ISBN 978-1-84550-646-9

Out of the Depths

Psalm 51

Martyn Lloyd-Jones

[This book] ... reveals Dr. Lloyd-Jones' compassion and concern for the spiritually lost. He aims to make known the saving power of Jesus Christ and to call men to repentance and faith. That driving passion marked Lloyd-Jones' preaching with urgency...here you find a surgeon at work bringing healing to his hearers.

Thabiti Anyabwile, Pastor,
First Baptist Church, Grand Cayman, Cayman Islands

If you are looking for understanding on repentance then turn to one of the classic passages in the Old Testament, Psalm 51. This Psalm takes us back in the life of David to when he committed adultery with Uriah's wife, Bathsheba. This sordid story is the backdrop to a moving study that gives readers a fuller understanding of the vital importance of repentance for Christians and non-Christian. *Out of the Depths* details the sinner's confession, helplessness and a central need. There is good news as Lloyd Jones shows that there is also deliverance and new life. This book will be a help to you if you are an earnest seeker after God who wants to take that first step on the road to salvation, and for the troubled Christian desiring to once again find the path to a restored relationship with God.

Introduced by Tullian Tchividjian

TRUE
HAPPINESS

PSALM 1

MARTYN
LLOYD-JONES

ISBN 978-1-84550-645-2

True Happiness

Psalm 1

MARTYN LLOYD-JONES

[This book is] ... filled with heart and hope ...possessing a rare combination (compared to much preaching today) of gravity and gladness, depth and delight, doctrine and devotion, precept and passion, truth and love. By God's grace you will find yourself (as I did) weeping over your sin, celebrating your forgiveness, and exalting in God's bigness. These sermons are intended to make you feel your desperation, cry out for deliverance, and celebrate your pardon.

Tullian Tchividjian, Senior Pastor,
Coral Ridge Presbyterian Church, Ft. Lauderdale, Florida

Everyone is in pursuit of happiness. Have you found it? Why not take a moment to stop, pause, consider and mediate on your relationship with the Creator and what He has done to save us. We don't have to go far to discover that in time of the psalmist, people were looking for happiness. The way to find it was to seek after the way of righteousness. Here Martyn Lloyd-Jones takes a look at Psalm 1 that is sure to cause readers to pause and think about their own lives. In these expository writings, this renowned preacher unveils the secrets of happiness and praise, and once again faithfully defines God's Word while speaking directly to the hearts of readers. Today's readers will be able to find answers to their quest for answers.

Introduced by Daniel Montgomery

LET EVERYBODY PRAISE THE LORD

PSALM 107

MARTYN LLOYD-JONES

ISBN 978-1-84550-685-8

Let Everybody Praise the Lord
Psalm 107

MARTYN LLOYD-JONES

Some doctors never go beyond the surface but Martyn Lloyd-Jones is surgical in his preaching speaking with clarity, weight and specificity to the urgent needs of the ailing human heart. A unifying theme in all his messages is a man pleading with his people to recognize the depths of their sin and pointing to the never ending depths of God's mercy in Christ.

Daniel Montgomery, Lead Pastor,
Sojourn Community Church, Louisville, Kentucky

As he expounds this wonderful psalm Dr Martyn Lloyd-Jones sees a great choir, drawn from the four corners of the earth, united in praising God. Using the Psalmist's vivid word-pictures he underlines the sheer grace of God who rescues sinners from the wilderness, frees them from prison, heals them from dreadful disease and saves them from a terrible storm. Throughout this superb exposition Dr. Martyn Lloyd-Jones show the profound difference between false and true religion. True Christianity always, and inevitably, leads to grateful and heart-felt praising of God 'for his goodness and for his wonderful works to the children of men.'

TRUTH UNCHANGED, UNCHANGING

MARTYN LLOYD-JONES

ISBN 978-1-84550-734-3

Truth Unchanged, Unchanging

Martyn Lloyd-Jones

When Lloyd-Jones points out the way in which men and women seek to legitimize their actions on the basis of what is natural or instinctive it feels as though he has been trolling the blogs and tweets of today. It is the timelessness and timeliness of his observations that give this book a prophetic edge.

Alistair Begg, Senior Pastor,
Parkside Church, Chagrin Falls, Ohio

In our world we see day by problems such as crime, exploitation, greed, proverty, pollution and war and often causes us to ask:

What is man?

What is wrong with the human race?

Today those who shape social policy often offer the wrong answers. Dr Lloyd-Jones takes us beyond human prejudices and provides us with a apologetic for the gospel. The doctor exposes these flaws in modern thinking, especially in the "scientific approach." He provides us with a penetrating diagnosis of the human condition and show decisively that the true remedy for our ills is in Jesus Christ - and Him alone. Truly every we need for salvation is found in Christ alone.

Evangelical Movement of Wales

The EMW seeks to help Christians and churches by:

- running children's camps and family conferences;
- providing theological training and events for ministers;
- running Christian bookshops and a conference centre;
- publishing magazines and books.

It works in both the Welsh and English languages.

Past issues of our magazines and sermons preached at our conferences are available on our website.

For further information, go to:

www.emw.org.uk

Christian Focus Publications

Our mission statement –

STAYING FAITHFUL

In dependence upon God we seek to impact the world through literature faithful to His infallible Word, the Bible. Our aim is to ensure that the Lord Jesus Christ is presented as the only hope to obtain forgiveness of sin, live a useful life and look forward to heaven with Him.

Our Books are published in four imprints:

CHRISTIAN
FOCUS

popular works including biographies, commentaries, basic doctrine and Christian living.

CHRISTIAN
HERITAGE

books representing some of the best material from the rich heritage of the church.

MENTOR

books written at a level suitable for Bible College and seminary students, pastors, and other serious readers. The imprint includes commentaries, doctrinal studies, examination of current issues and church history.

CF4•K

children's books for quality Bible teaching and for all age groups: Sunday school curriculum, puzzle and activity books; personal and family devotional titles, biographies and inspirational stories – Because you are never too young to know Jesus!

Christian Focus Publications Ltd,
Geanies House, Fearn, Ross-shire,
IV20 1TW, Scotland, United Kingdom.
www.christianfocus.com